The Language of Lockdown

Lockdown at Nine by Lily Gregory (Aged 9)

It is currently week nine in Lockdown. We are still unable to attend school or visit other people's homes. The only time I am leaving home is to go on our daily walk, adventuring through the woods. Living thorough Lockdown, I have experienced lots of mixed emotions.

Before finishing school, due to Lockdown, I felt very worried and anxious about the Coronavirus. I feared my family might catch the virus and there was lots of talk at school about what might happen. Finishing school and staying at home, made me feel safe. It is hard to not see my family, who I would usually see all the time. I really want to hug them but I know that if I really want to keep them safe, then I must stay away.

My Dad is also a policeman and I feel concerned because he is still going to work every day. He is putting himself at risk each day. I know he has to do this to keep the community safe. Watching the news makes me feel more worried, hearing about the virus and hearing how many people have died. I feel tearful, for their families and the doctors and nurses caring for them.

Despite all this, there have been positive times. I have learned lots of new skills through this time, such as; making loom band bracelets, making pom-pom animals and learning to crochet. Normally, I wouldn't be able to learn these skills because I would be at school and wouldn't have the time. I am trying to work hard from home, keeping up with my school work. I also feel lucky because I get to spend more time with my family and my younger sister; I have even helped to teach her to ride her bike without stabilisers. I will cherish this memory.

We also have more time now to eat as a family and we have found different ways to entertain ourselves. We have had movie night, walks in our beautiful local area, afternoon tea and barbeques in the sunshine. I celebrated my ninth birthday during lockdown and my family visited but could only look through the window.

We also celebrated VE day, people had street parties but we stayed in and kept safe. Instead, I decorated the house and made scones for my Dad, ready for when he finished his shift. I have also used technology to keep in touch with my friends and had dancing lessons on Zoom.

Hopefully, lockdown will end soon and I look forward to seeing my friends and family, friends coming over and going back to school. I know that I am one of the lucky ones, because we are all safe and healthy.

Lockdown in Nerja 2020 by Carole Moore

COVID-19 has arrived in Spain!
We have to stay in, which is a bit of a pain
But reading the facts, it's the right thing to do
To keep it from spreading, to us and to you.

DAY 1 was a novelty, just watching TV
That soon became boring, so it's not to be!
Now on DAY 5, friends are starting to chat
Using their Facebook, and sometimes Whatsapp!

We've watched people singing, and telling a joke
And even cooking breakfast......I know that Scots bloke!
Chopping his fruit, to put in his dishes
Waiting to say,' Good Morning' to the missus.

At 8 in the evening, we all go and stand
Out on our balconies, clapping our hands.
Applauding the medics, and the police too
Thanking them both, for all that they do.

Lockdown in Nerja 2020 by Carole Moore cont.

Some narrow minded people, who live in the UK
Have been queuing in shops, and not keeping away
They've bought pasta galore, and toilet rolls too
They're stacked to the ceiling, behind the white loo!

We've another 2 weeks, or maybe it's more
To stay behind doors....now it's the law!
So keep entertaining us, I'm a great fan
Let's stay connected, as much as we can.

We all said we'd all party, when we get the all clear
But let's drink to the families, who have lost someone dear
And 'Cheers!' to the medics, and supermarket staff
Not forgetting our Facebook friends, who gave us a laugh!

Monday 18th May 2020........Out Out!!
by Carole Moore

Today is the first day
That we can go out!
For a drink on the terrace...
'Hurray' we all shout
A table of ten,
Is the most that we can have
And you have to wear a mask,
When visiting the lav!

It's beers all round,
And sunglasses too
One of each colour,
Like red or green and blue
Catching up on news,
Of the weeks that have passed
We're all necking beer,
As if it were our last!

Swapping our recipes,
Of cakes, that we've made
And titles of boxsets,
From Netflix we've paid
Jigsaws and novels,
And a Zoom family quiz
And videos from Tik Tok.......
Whatever that is!

Monday 18th May 2020........Out Out!!
by Carole Moore cont.

We've missed our good friends,
By staying indoors
But to keep us safe,
We obeyed the Spanish laws
It doesn't seem so bad,
Now that we're free
We have been the lucky ones,
You and me

Only one more week,
And we move to Phase 2
We can walk with a friend,
Or maybe it's two
The restaurants can open,
50% inside
Don't forget the table distance,
2m wide

Let's spare a thought,
For businesses that closed
And support the ones now open....
I need to buy some clothes!!
So this summer will be quiet,
We know that's a fact
It's called the 'New Norm'....
Oh and EasyJet was hacked!

Mary Jean Topping by Tony Topping

My mam's recently changed her name, not in a big way to us she's always Mam or Mum, but she's gone from telling people her name's Jean Topping to saying her name is Mary Jean Topping. This is reasonable as that's her full name but it can be a bugger when you're looking for her in a hospital bed. Still when you are 86 years old you can do as you please.

My mam has had it tough over the last few years, to be honest she's not had an easy life bringing up five children with her husband Joe and she also looked after my grandfather and uncle when her mother died. But she wouldn't change a thing and she loves her family and we love her. She does love a party though.

Last August my son Martin got married and she was so looking forward to going to the wedding. Sadly she spent that day and the following weeks very ill in a hospital. Thankfully she made a full recovery and despite some walking difficulties was able to enjoy little trips out and a bingo night once a week with local senior members. Then like a black cloud blocking the sun came the virus.

Everything was put on hold once more and the family events she loved so much were derailed again. It got her down a bit, it got her family down even more but her indomitable spirit shone through and as she would always say "You just have to get on with it" She did that and more when dad died 12 years ago and she's lived alone ever since.

If I can I'd like to take you back to the mid 1970s when the council house we lived in could have used a revolving door. It was a hive of activity always full of relations and friends the walls resounded with laughter and good cheer. Christmas was the highlight of the year but not the only one on show. Royal weddings and engagements called for dressing up, bunting and fizzy bottles with exploding corks. She also loved St Patrick's Day being so proud of her Irish ancestors.

This year she spent St Patrick's day alone apart from the closest members of her family who visited her from the safety of the garden gate for a brief moment. It didn't stop her dressing up in the emerald green though, she loves putting her outfits on as much as she likes a slice of cake and she likes cake a lot.

Mary Jean Topping by Tony Topping cont.

VE Day was no different and she was decked out in her patriotic colours with a smile a mile wide. I took a photograph of her from the bottom of the garden and my sister Kathryn sent it to the Wigan Observer who kindly put it in their tributes to that wonderful day that rewarded us with so much sunshine. Mam was so proud she rang everyone she knew to tell them she was in the local paper. It went a long way to lifting the disappointment of missing out on another family get together.

We, the family, can promise our mam one thing though; when this pandemic is over we shall hold the party to end all parties to celebrate the life of Mary Jean Topping and the love she gave us all.

Wigan is Dreaming by Donna Gowland

Warm hearts melting cold steel skies,
Capped heads cheering, hot meat pies.
Wool spun fingers, coal face grit,
The greens of Alexander park, kids keeping fit.
The loud roars of King Street bold and bright,
Hungover by day but golden by night.
Cabs from North Western, fights by the Gate,
Buzzing at Bingo Gail's running late.
There's a groom at the Atrium smoking with fear,
And the sun is an egg yoke dipped into the Pier.
Hoods bent over Mab's Cross over screens, perched on bikes,
Spark flashes of nature on their flesh and the spikes.
Pull into the station, we surrender the walls,
Place new tags by old names, those famous mint balls.
What I'd give for them right now, or a pie in a barm,
Or a walk round the shops, with their glistening charm.
What I'd give to see wrinkled hands supping their ale,
Or the girls from the centre still waiting for Gail.
Wigan, you're sleeping and dream while you might,
For you'll flourish again and all will be reet.

Are You Talking To Me by Eileen Hutchings

Are you talking to me
Born in 43
Midst all the bombs
The shortages and songs
You're telling me
We'll soon be free
Free to choose what
Now there's a spot of bother
For you to consider
So you change one small word
Will it change our world
Of staying indoors
For our good of course
But if you had done
Working as one
Shut down our small island
Let us be crammed
Surrounded by sand
But safe and secure
In our little homes
Letting no one converge
Rejecting a surge
On our precious shores
But we are surviving
Each night and each day
By staying away
From those we hold dear
From friends and relations
No celebrations

Except
On screen and on phone
In contact whilst being alone
We exchange all our news
Argue our views
But we always agree
One day we'll be free
To kiss and to cuddle
In one family huddle
So we'll do as he says
Plus be kind in our ways
Look after each other
No fuss and no bother
But hey we're alive
We will survive
This covid-19
For we are seen as a battling nation
Each one to their station
To join the fight
To exit the plight
We find ourselves in
So keep on repeating
Mr Johnson is "leading"
So
Stay alert
Control the virus
Save lives

My Lucky Sock Are Waiting
by Katherine McDermott

They're folded neatly in the top drawer.
In my match day drawer as I call it. With my shirt and scarf.
These items are kept separate from all my other clothes.
These are special.
All neatly folded ready and waiting to be worn for the next game.
They've not been worn for weeks.
They still smell of Surf Tropical Lilly from the last game I watched my team play on some illegal streaming site on the 12th March.
That seems like a lifetime ago to me.
The endless stream of time that lingers from one day to the next.
Hopeless.
I'm hopeless. I'm not the only one.
All football fans are.
You see our concept of time is different to everyone else's.
We don't do years we do seasons.
August to May.
Each game is broken down into individual component parts for which I calculate the
X amount of minutes travelling to and from the game.
(1 hour 30 minutes for me to be exact).
90 minutes for the game.
45 minutes for each half played plus
X amount of stoppage time before the ref blows the final whistle
(also known as Fergie time)
Average that out over several games in the week for the various cup competitions.
Or, if your club doesn't have many competitions to compete in
You can still have another match to look forward to.
We navigate our time according to football fixtures and televised matches and commentary on Radio 5 Live.

My Lucky Socks Are Waiting
by Katherine McDermott cont.

We define our own life's success during the season by our team's position in the table.
By goals saved, goals conceded, matches won and lost and defensive records.
We measure our week by how well our team has played during the week;
If a player is injured or playing utter rubbish.
Player statistics for assists, passes, goals scored, miles run during the game.
Concrete. Definite. Facts
And if we lose then we can always say "there's always the next game".
I know there will always be things that are unexplainable.
That are a complete mystery that not even a priest or the bible has an answer for;
Such as how has Phil Jones survived 16 transfer windows?
(No one has yet found an answer to this mystery)
But this -
This time now?
This is something else.
We have no idea of when the season will finish.
When the new season will start.
And will the fans be allowed to be there?
The thought of football with no fans, no congregation, no singing, not standing
shoulder to shoulder with my fellow Spartans, well –
I can't bear to even think about it.
We share the tears. We share the cheer.
We share the heart ache. We share the pain and the anger.
It's what we do.
But now there's nothing.
It's all a muddle.
But what I do know -
All I know is -
My lucky socks are waiting.

Springtime in Lockdown by Sue Healy

Almost every day since lockdown began my daughter and I have walked up through the plantations to Haigh Hall. Haigh Hall is our local stately home that occupies an elevated position over the town. The plantations is the deciduous woodland that lines the route from the west. There are several entrance points and we're fortunate enough to live opposite one of them.

In March the trees were bare and there was little ground cover. Over these 10+ weeks we've seen snowdrops, then wild garlic leaves appeared. We snipped some of those a few times a week and used them in salads, to make wild garlic butter for jacket potatoes, in curries and stir fries, the list was long. We also cut some for friends and delivered in a socially distant manner. In some instances this involved hanging a bag on a doorknob.

This has been a gorgeous year for blossom, though we saw with sadness that a few trees on Swinley Lane were cut down after blossoming.

As the wild garlic flowers appeared so did the bluebells. They lasted ages. Beautiful.

We saw the chestnut trees bud first. Some of those trees must be 200 years old. Each species followed in turn and now there are innumerable shades and shapes of green.

The whole way through this there have been people walking, running and cycling the paths to and from the Hall, always keeping a respectful distance. Up above the hall are the shops, cafes and playgrounds. These have all been closed and that area has largely been deserted, even on the sunniest days. Often we were completely alone in the sunshine and felt very fortunate. We've seen deer, heard woodpeckers, noticed how many more butterflies and bees there have been. The skies have been clear with only the very occasional vapour trail. It's difficult to avoid the conclusion that this lack of air traffic has contributed to the sparling clear air we've enjoyed.

Springtime in Lockdown by Sue Healy cont.

The fountain in the pond has been running the whole time. I'm sure this is because it's part of the cleanliness and life of the pond. We've seen the waterlilies spread and flower, the frogspawn hatch and the tadpoles grow. Nature seems to have been running riot. I wonder if that's the case, or is it that we've slowed down and paid attention? I've never in my entire life, as a child or an adult, watched a spring at close quarters in the way I have this one. I think, hope actually, that it's changed something in me. Enforced rest has been so valuable as has time to think and reflect.

Sadly, though I fully recognise the awful circumstances that have led to this experience, I think this time of stillness is over. Yesterday was Bank Holiday Monday, May 25th. There was a change. People had driven to the hall rather than making their way under their own steam. It was busy. There was a scattering of trash that was sad and puzzling to see. There was an underlying buzz that has been absent. I wonder if anything will have changed.

We've been privileged to have this time and this access to a beautiful place at a beautiful time.

I hope we can keep hold of some of it.

Stay At Home by Debra Biggs

Stay at home they said
There's a killer on the loose
Stay at home they said
Lock yourselves away
No hugs for your mum, no kisses for your grandkids
Stay at home they said
Hundreds of thousands are dead and more are dying
Don't let this silent killer in
Empty shelves in supermarkets
The selfishness of people brought out by panic
Who will survive this sci fi film nightmare that is now reality?
Stay at home they said
No birthday celebrations, no weddings, no family gatherings
Stay at home they said, pray and hope for survival
Is this the world's way of saying enough is enough?
Then out of the darkness a glimmer of hope
Rainbows in windows and chalked onto pavements
8pm clapping for our brave key workers
Each one making the sacrifice for everyone else
The 100yr old pensioner marching to victory
Raising the country's spirits
Neighbours helping neighbours
Birdsong heard clearly in every garden around the country
Nature is recovering as the world hibernates
Stay at home they said, just a little while longer
Stay at home, stay safe

Stronger by Katie Bilsborough

Want to see your family?
FaceTime will have to do.

Need a Sunday roast?
Pubs will deliver it to you.

It's your best friend's birthday?
Have a party over Zoom.

Schools are closed?
Well never mind, we've got Google Classroom.

Exercise?
You can go out, but only once a day.

Weekly shop?
Tesco's fine, just stay two metres away.

Fed up?
I know, but please just wait a little longer.

Are things normal?
No, but we'll come out of this stronger.

Isolated War by Niamh Williams

Silence always deafens
Walls forever confine
Time slowly passes
The world out there, I no longer recognise

Distressing in moments
We are all isolated in grief
Watching, begging, praying for mercy
Searching for relief

Darkness prevails
And yet more pain
The ominous power
Of a viral reign

Tiresome nights
Apprehensive for the next day
Enduring this hurt
That no soul should have to obey

Life in Lockdown by Niamh Williams

Our lives are different now as we all stay inside
We take turns looking at data and how many have died
There was absolute carnage to stock up the freezer and kitchen cupboards too
People even rationed the toilet roll when they went to the loo

Boris closed schools and the cinemas too
Without shops and bars, we all had to make do
Trade was lost and shares plummeted down
All caused by that virus with the wicked crown

Most nights my family sit on the couch watching the telly
Brews in our hands and food in our belly
The news yet again has one continuous story
So, I turn to my phone to find something that won't bore me

The reaction by global leaders was not united
Some shrugged it off others were foresighted
And yet the virus spread, the leaders thought it would
be over quickly if they did what they could.

How Lucky Am I in Coronavirus Times? by Nigel Green

How lucky am I to be alive in these challenging Coronavirus times, unlike many who have tragically succumbed to a deadly demise?

How lucky am I to have a father alive, at the age of 95, he plays music, paints, exercises and reads and then he takes his ease?

How lucky am I to have a clean and tidy house and car and nothing I need to do really, except listen to the birds singing now their songs can be heard more clearly?

How lucky am I to be able to sit and admire the flowers in my back garden, the result of many hours of hard work but a pleasure to beholden?

How lucky am I to observe the changing landscape and seasons, sculpted by farmers and nature and for other less important reasons?

How lucky am I to be able to ride my bike on quiet country lanes, less cars on our roads means we are much safer and refrained?

How lucky am I to be supported by a loving wife who understands my needs, and is always looking after family and friends to help them succeed?

How lucky am I to be able to use social media to keep in touch with my children, the youngest change so quickly – when will we meet again, grandchildren?

How lucky am I to be involved in organisations that promote physical activity, to share ideas and challenge practice to promote lifelong physical activity?

How Lucky Am I In Coronavirus Times? by Nigel Green cont.

How lucky am I to be able to keep in touch with friends and family throughout the world, using social media platforms to share what others have seen or heard?

How lucky am I to be able to sit in the sun and ponder on how life has progressed to here, to recollect on past experiences and look forward to another year?

How lucky am I to have sufficient food and toilet rolls plus a supply of beer, and wine to help me feel fine, for at least another year?

How lucky am I to be in a position to help neighbours collecting medicines and food or mowing the lawn, and to marvel at the unpolluted skies in the evening or at dawn?

How lucky am I to have shop workers, delivery drivers and a host of key workers, prepared to work to help everyone get through this challenging time, there are no shirkers?

How lucky am I to be able to feed the pheasants in the morning, see the birds bathe in the pond, and watch the frog spawn and transform, all summer long?

How lucky am I to have doctors, nurses and carers to look after all who need, their help and experience puts us all at ease?

In these challenging Coronavirus times, it is good to reflect on what we have that is precious, the future experiences that are yet to come, stay safe, stay at home and protect the NHS.

**Lockdown Walks 1
by Martin Holden**

Big Hearts in a Small Town by Jack McKenna

The world has come to a screeching halt and I've been dragged from the city back home. Belligerent car horns beeping and boisterous crowds buzzing seem but a dim echo in my ears; now eager starlings call my liminal mind to action.

Ah, back in this small, unchanged world. This world where the rows of short brick houses leave the blue sky free to stretch above; where the cobbled streets wind between the woodlands; where everyone carries that same, bold accent and the town is busied in bursts of dog walking, shopping, and nights to drink away. I shut the door behind me and fix my cap, the sun glares above. "'Ello!", comes in its usual warmth; my neighbour painting his fence, wiping the sweat from his brow. His daughter's just had a baby, what a time, eh? "She's alreet though, what about you?"

"Oh, back from the city," – a touch of bitterness on my tongue, "doing well though, nice to be back I suppose."

"It'll do you good lad," he waves goodbye. I walk out of the cul-de-sac and turn, I'm astounded by the smiles, nods, 'ellos and alreets, that come my way.

Painting the fences or cleaning their cars with their sun-kissed faces, everyone on my street is busy on this weekend morning. The houses are radiant, their fronts sparkling clean and their windows rainbowed with children's handprints.

I pull out of my street - a jogger runs by, then another! Panting their inexperience away in old football shirts and baggy tops. It seems my street was not alone, the rows of connected houses are alive – glowing in the sun, conversations sound over the freshly painted fences and the smell of freshly cut grass saturates the air.

A mother and a young girl drop a large shopping bag in front of a doorstep, knock, and step away – I slow my pace to watch. The mother holds back her daughter as she tries to walk open armed towards the door. It opens slowly to an older, tired looking woman in a nurse's uniform emerging from the dark. Her exhaustion is swept away by her and her families' raised hands. They cheer and exchange joyfully. "The hospitals a bit overrun, but no, I'm doing well thank you." They're glad to hear – "I'll be okay thank you"

Big Hearts in a Small Town by Jack McKenna cont.

I slip onto the overgrown path that leads me towards the heath. The ash trees cast a soft shadow which the sun only pierces in slices. I can't help but think of the city, the towering shadows and the barren streets, the sharp glances across pavements. Now that tomorrow has dissolved along with yesterday, the city seems much less alive, the sky spliced by skyscrapers seem much less appealing to me.

I come out onto the street to the sound of the canal rushing below and a pigeon cooing above. The old overgrown field radiates and the grass hovers in the still breeze. I wind up the road, past the ghosts of collieries, back into the small world.

An ambulance soars past, sirens blaring! – those busied on their porches pause for a moment's solemnity. Nature becomes silent too. The pigeon pauses on top of a fence. The grave realisation sets in and time truly seems to stand still. The tired nurse springs to mind, the families painting their rainbow spirit across their windows – I'm reminded about that oppressive, invisible cloud that looms above.

I walk up to the heath, realising how each ambulance trip fills a hospital bed. How each bed fills a family's heart with sorrow. I arrive at the heath, thinking how much this world is suffering, and gaze around. A dog soars across the field chasing a ball, an elderly couple walks along the path as a younger couple steps aside, joggers run by, a vicar speaks warmly to an elderly woman across her drive, a young boy sits by his parked bicycle after delivering a birthday present to an old man, holding onto the doorway. The ambulance's sirens fade away into the distance – all of these people heard it, yet they all carry on wearing their smiles and helping each other out. Everyone has their task on this sunny weekend day –

Perhaps this small world isn't as small as I once thought.

A Winter's Week by Marie Beattie

On Monday there was a soaking sleet
Which left no mark upon our street

Tuesday was a day of snow steadily drifting down
Muffling the sound around

Wednesday there was a patter of rain
It glugged as it left the gutter, and gushed out of the drain

Thursday, brought hours of furious wind, a giant fist, that pushed people to and fro
As they struggled to get where they wanted to go

Friday the fog made it difficult to see
For sailors in peril on the sea

Saturday the ice made ponds and rivers
glisten like so many mirrors

Sunday the sun broke through beaming down on me and you
Cheering us up making us smile
Albeit for a very short while

The Sound of Drumming (Abridged)
by Robin Long

There's a drum kit in the corner of my spare bedroom and it's gathering dust. In February 2020 I retired from work and was looking forward to getting to grips with my drums and the lockdown meant I had no excuses.

But I got distracted by an idea that I got from the toilet of an hotel in the Lake District where they had covered the walls with old maps of the area. I endeavoured to copy this effect with old Michelin road atlases of France. You only realise how big France is when you pull apart two copies of the road atlas and try to stick them together on your walls like a huge jigsaw. Even though the maps looked identical, a 2013 and a 2017, they are not, it's far from perfect but I maybe should have planned it better. The Creuse, where my house is, hides behind the wardrobe. The village of Lye, where I visited my in-laws' cottage for over 20 years is behind the sofa bed and Belfort where my good friend Helen lives didn't even fit on. I've had to stick that in the window recess. At least from my desk I can see some of my favourite places. Alpe d'Huez is to the left of the window, the Col du Tourmalet is just below the window ledge and Mont Ventoux, the Giant of Provence, features to the right.

My house is above the window. The drums managed to lose a bit of their dust but only because I had to move them.

The worst thing about lockdown for me was my grandchildren. There's nothing wrong with my grandchildren. They are wonderful. It's just that I only know one of them. Having been away before it all started I haven't seen grandson number one, at the time of writing, for about twelve weeks. Grandson number two was born on 29th March and I haven't seen him at all. I know there are people who have suffered, are suffering, much more than not seeing their new grandchild but it doesn't make it any easier. On the plus side, he is a tiny baby and doesn't do anything yet. He won't remember not seeing his grandparents for the first couple of months of his life. Unless this drags on and I don't get to see him before graduation. With grandson number one I have had to be more creative. During video chats with his mum I started reading Spike Milligan poems to him, which he loves. This progressed to making short videos of me reciting silly verse and posting them online so others can get some enjoyment too. All this distracting me from dusting off the drums

We are all dealing with this in our own way. Some have taken the opportunity to become more creative while many haven't. Some have taken the opportunity to post their new abilities on social media as if to shame us all into action while many haven't. Others have taken this rare chance to slow down and take stock, ignore what others are doing and tackle the issue as they see fit. Some have done that with a jumbo bar of milk chocolate and a litre of vodka. To do or not to do? That is the question and it matters not one tiny iota whether or not you have, as long as you have got through it.

Learning the drums isn't the only thing I have long wanted to make more time for. Having a little maison secondaire in France, I feel the need and desire to learn more of the language and this I am doing albeit rather slowly. By little I mean little. You may have spoken to other people who say they have a "little" place in France then find out it's a medieval chateau in 20 hectares or a converted mill with 12 bedrooms and a working water wheel. Mine really is small, a one up, one down with a kitchen on the side and a yard the size of a postage stamp but it's a chateau to me.

I have also spent more time reading, completing crosswords and puzzles, all those little things that are good for the slightly ageing brain. The miles on the bike have shot up too. But the one thing I have always told myself I will do one day is write. I heard a writer recounting that many people say to her that they wish they could write. Her reply is always, "You can." So I have and the irony is that writing about not playing the drums has given me yet another excuse to not play the drums.

There's a drum kit in the corner of my spare bedroom and it's gathering dust.

Things We Appreciate by Joshua Smith

Things we will learn how much we appreciate:

A simple party
A day of school
A dog called Marley
A day at the pool

These are somethings we learn to appreciate:

Throwing a stick
Going to church on a Sunday
Meeting with Mick
Going for a coffee with somebody

Now we appreciate them and don't take them for granted:

Visiting the mill
Winning an award
Climbing a hill
Now we'll go on the holidays we couldn't afford!

These are the things we will always appreciate.

Thoughts During Lockdown
by Joan Brickley (Aged 80)

Here I am in my own Bubble. For nine whole weeks I have been in 'Lockdown.'
I'm 80 years old and have been told that I am vulnerable.
So my world consists of my house and my garden.

Whilst I am in my Bubble, I feel safe and can shut out all thoughts of Covid and all of its dangers.

Sometimes, things try to break into my Bubble causing me to leave it's comforting safety and pull me out into reality and all it's madness.

On TV I see doctors and nurses looking weary, lorry drivers frightened to go home to their family, living in their cabs unable to get a shower or a cup of coffee.
Store workers trying to deal with frustrated customers.
People who have lost loved ones.
Then, I have my 'wobble.' My heart sinks.
I hear myself saying a prayer.

Then I hear my phone ring.
'Hello, how are you?' asks a familiar voice. Someone I can speak to.
'I'm ok' is my answer and, for a while, worries have disappeared as we both talk about our thoughts, our anxieties but, also, the little funny things that have happened since last we met and we find, from deep inside, there appears a smile that leads to a laugh. For those few minutes, life is 'normal' once again.
We say 'Goodbye' and promise to keep in touch.

I glance over to an armchair near me and my eyes rest on a cushion which shows a picture of my grandchildren. It seems so long since I saw them and gave them a cuddle. I can't count how many times in the day I look at it and feel that they are here.

Then, suddenly, I 'creep' back into the relative safety of my Bubble where there is room for my knitting, painting, sketching and reading and where, for a while, I can shut out the virus filled world until the next time my Bubble bursts.

Invisible Enemy by Lynda Harrison

2020 the world went on pause,
A killer virus being the cause.
Viruses on their own can't spread,
Without our movement the virus is dead.
The sooner that we all stay in,
Healing and eradication begin.

The lockdown had reduced the curve,
Those who have obeyed have shown they
care.
Let's continue in the very same vein,
To deny the virus is the aim.

The keyworkers have kept our country on
green,
Without them where would we have been?
They've proved beyond doubt the working
man's worth,
They truly are the salt of the earth.

Individuals doing their bit,
Making PPE and sewing kit.
This is what make our country the best,
Those that can, helping the rest.

Captain Tom stole the heart of the nation,
He did it with love and determination.
The walking will have been hard for a man
of his years,
But he carried on going and brought us to
tears.

He demonstrated all that is good,
And many contributed, if they could.
If we pull together we have such might,
That's the best weapon we have in this fight.

Those who think Covid can't catch you,
And if it does it's just the flu.
You still have time to get it right,
With your help we have even more might.

And when this is over we mustn't forget,
And bad employers will regret,
As we the public vote with our feet,
Bad employers must never repeat.
Many employers have done the right thing,
They are the ones whose praises we'll sing.

To the families who've lost and whose lives
have been shattered,
To each and all your loss leaves you tattered.
Our deepest condolences we send,
With a hug and prayer to help you mend.

Invisible Enemy by Lynda Harrison cont.

As men and women with brains as their power,
Spend much of their time, hour after hour.
Vaccine and medication are their goals,
With the hope of saving many more souls.

Here's to the day when they triumph and win,
Then world healing can begin.

When this juncture in time is reached,
The lessons learned must keep up meek.
The world can run at a much slower pace,
As we all learn what's good to embrace.
Life doesn't have to be lived like a race,
We don't need to run at a constant face pace

Let's take a step back and enjoy what matters,
Simple things in life are usually the pleasure.
We've seen such kindness and the strengh of many
Let's live in peace and total harmony.

Here's to live and the pleasure of living,
Let's hope this experience keps us all giving.

Lockdown Walks 1b
by Martin Holden

A Story About A Virus by Amelie Leggott (Aged 6)

This is the story about a virus that started,
And all the people had to stay parted,
The world had a really big fight,
To make everything right,
We went on walks,
And had lots of talks,
Sometimes we got sad,
Which made us feel a bit mad,
But other times we felt happy,
Because we thought about seeing all of our grandparents, Nanna and Pappy.

Thirteen Minutes from Home by Ian Whiteley

I was thirteen minutes from home
On a warm April day
Bumping my way through a crowd
The future a lifetime away
There were cars revving their engines
As they crawled along the street
kids were playing in gardens
And getting under everyone's feet

Just for a second I paused
As I turned into Pandemic Close
As the noise fell away like a corpse
And the postman turned into a ghost
The cars all ground to a halt
The planes fell out of the sky
The children screamed to be let out
An old man started to cry

I was overtaken with guilt
That I would prefer it that way
Empty streets and less people and traffic
To ruin a clear spring day
I breathed in the cool clear air
I listened to birds in the trees
At last I could hear myself think
And my thoughts ran away on the breeze

I was seven minutes from home
When reality thundered back in
And that Utopia I'd seen in a vision
Disappeared like it never had been
And the crowd gathered round and exhaled
And on their breath there was pain
And I knew in my heart what I'd seen
I would surely see once again

The day I stepped into a dream
Prepared me for what was to come
Half a century away in the future
I would remember where I'd travelled from
I was two minutes from midnight
And all of us would bemoan what we lost
Utopia isn't always an Eden
Sometimes it brings Hell as a cost

33

Coronavirus Lockdown
by Ember MacNamara (Aged 6)

It's boring, not able to go to the park, absolutely boring.

House too clean,

Streets are almost deserted but too peopley on walks.

It's boring all over the world

All my lessons are about soap

I miss my Dadda working at the hospital

+ Timmy Cat.

Miss my proper friends, I can't see them.

Lockdown makes me feel sadness.

I wish it all wasn't real, wish it was all just a dream.

Wish all the kids where as lucky as me with lovely parents and caring people and family who love me.

Elegy for Lost Homes by Ian Whiteley

Another day has come and passed
Left pain and sadness in its wake
The seconds, minutes, hours amassed
The sun will give the moon will take
The distant friends the loved ones lost
Amid the times of dread disease
Each family will count the cost
And curse the name of days like these

And yet the sky was clearest blue
I wrote a poem, sang a song
We danced together me and you
and talked and laughed the whole day long
We passed by others in the street
And noticed them unlike before
We went online our friends to meet
We valued moments, wanted more

Tomorrow is another day
The sun will rise and set again
Some will win and others will pay
Each loss rebalanced with a gain
These times will pass as others did
We may look back on them and say
We were alive we never hid
They could not take our dreams away

35

Lockdown Life by Isla Davenport (Aged 10)

There is something going on and we are not allowed to leave,
There is something going on and it is hard to believe.

Everywhere is shut and that means we can't buy a Krispy creme doughnut!

Whilst talking to my friends on the phone I just want to leave our home!

I've spent lots of time with my family,
We've done lots of fun things,
We've been for walks and played outside and done lots of baking!

It's been quite an unusual time,
I've missed my friends and going to school,
I even had a lockdown birthday which was different but rather cool!

I guess I've liked our lockdown life but I can't wait to see my family and friends,
I'll give them all the biggest hug when social distancing ends.

It Is by Janice Barker

It is the eerie silence deserted city streets.
It is the ghostly stillness of a theatre's empty seats.
It is the gentle breeze on a kids abandoned playground.
It is deafening quiet where child laughter should be found.
It is the rows and rows of resting planes.
It is the still running but half empty trains.
It is the sound of a siren as an ambulance speeds.
It is a moment of reflection and inspiring good deeds.
It is the person who will live and the one who dies.
It is a symbol of truth in a myriad of lies.
It is thinking of the people on the front line of this fight.
It is thankful they strive on each day and every night.
It is fearful of the unseen killer stealing many lives.
It is mindful there's no pattern to who dies and who survives.
It is content to be in splendid isolation.
It is doing one's bit with the rest of this nation.
It is the whispering voices of poor souls taken.
It is certain one day from this we will waken.
It is the sadness felt by the families of many.
It is looking for a reason, but it cannot find any.
It is hoping that one day it will all be in the past.
It is praying new found likenesses will always last.
It is the voice of millions or of just one.
It is the end of tragedy and a new world won!

Open the Box by Jacqueline Pemberton

I am making a memory box
Something to encapsulate
This time of isolation.
A two foot square creation.
With a combination lock.
My container is lined with
poetry
The dominant theme: COVD19
Like blood the words flow easily
Once you find a vein.
I've tried to avoid clichés
Find different synonyms for
loneliness.
I have a bundle of birthday
cards
Bound together with promises
to party,
when this is all over.
Homemade cards from
grandchildren,
The red paint of their
fingerprints
Smudged along the borders,
Giant kisses tumbling off the
page.
Photographs of our missing
months,

Their games and lessons in the
garden,
Rainbows at their window.
A selfie before the neighbour's
dog
Drove me to distraction
Mementos from my daily walks:
A green leaf, a delicate primrose
And two painted pebbles:
'This will pass'.

Thank you N.H.S'
There are a few things I can't yet
include:
Masks, gloves, disinfectant wipes
And the last drops of sanitising
lotion.
I've collected a few headlines:
Covid Virus will change the
World Permanently
UN Warns World faces worst
crisis since W.W.2
A bubble graph to show the
latest curve
And how one person can infect a
hundred more
My calendar for March torn off,
Crossings out of all my
gallivants
Replaced by new enclosed
words:
Zoom, house party, Face time,
Telephone appointments with
my doctor,
Everything that avoids touch.
May, June, July, August....
The rest of the year still
Hangs in the balance.

To You, Who Gave Everything by Jeff Dawson

To you, who gave everything...

To you, with your empty words,
hollow promises and lies
To you, who ignored simple orders
to stay at home, just stay inside
To you, who scam the vulnerable
exploiting their struggle and plight
And to you, the perpetrators of abuse
the fear you create, is all we despise

You gave nothing, absolutely nothing
In our darkest hours, this tragic time

But to you, who kept the country running
you have our love, you have our pride
To you, who deliver essential goods
and the thousands of miles you drive
To you, who stack the shelves,
the shop workers on the front line
And to you who stayed at home
Clapping for carers on Thursday nights

To you, delivering post or emptying bins
the length and breadth of the land
To you, in communities supporting folk
who need that helping hand
To you, the volunteers and key workers
together, you're making a stand
Selfless actions fighting an enemy
Not one of us really understands

And to every one of you, caring for the sick
every single hour, risking your own lives
Never shirking your duties once
despite the danger you might find
Yes you, you who gave everything
You gave us hope in these worrying times
Our hearts are filled with gratitude
We owe you all our lives...

Jeff Dawson is also known as
 Punk poet Jeffarama!

39

And Maybe...by Amy Green

And maybe during this lockdown,
whilst isolated and trapped,
we'll take a moment to just
stop.
And think.

And maybe we'll finally start to listen
to the sweet birds tweeting,
And observe the fragile butterfly wings
fluttering through the blossoming flowers,
And be engulfed by the smell of oak trees
standing magnificently,
So that nature is embedded within us...

And maybe we'll embrace our natural
beauty without the desire to impress,
And consume less paraphernalia and
material possessions for comfort,
And disregard our self-indulgent selfies
and feeling inadequate,
So that internal beauty is celebrated...

And maybe we'll actively communicate
with our vulnerable neighbours,
And cling to our grandparents' hands
a little tighter with pulsating love,
And squeeze our parents closer
to feel protected in their arms,
So that affection is oozing from us...

And maybe we'll embrace our friends with
a renewed hug of love that feels raw,
And sip ice cold beers and clink
our glasses as we unite in pubs,
And feel the roar of a stadium and be
electrified by rumbling music at concerts,
So that togetherness is alive...

And maybe we'll walk triumphantly
to the peak of stunning mountains,
And dip our toes into meandering streams
that glisten in the sunlight,
And stare intently at the dazzling stars
whilst dreaming of new adventures,
So that wanderlust is thriving...

And maybe we'll consciously write more
heartfelt letters to be delivered,
And admire the compassion that flows
from a carer's gentle touch,
And not judge the homeless or refugees
who have lost all hope,
So that tolerance is growing within us...

And maybe we'll genuinely respect how
our beloved children need their teachers,
And smile more at the worn-out
supermarket workers,
And respect our doctors and nurses
who are selflessly risking everything,
So that appreciation is glowing from us...

And Maybe...by Amy Green cont.

And maybe we'll carefully observe the
delicate fingers of a newborn baby,
And relish the moment when a
belly laugh erupts from an innocent child,
And notice how the hands and feet of
lovers can be entwined as one,
So that love is consuming everything...

And maybe out of the shackles of chaos,
out of the desperation of darkness
And overwhelming fear,
We will ignite.
And let an unconditional,
Transformative and
Pure love burn.

Walls by Amy Green

The stale,
intimidating walls
stare at me
relentlessly
tormenting me,
teasing me,
trapping me,
twisting my every thought,
puncturing my freedom,
smothering my escape,
isolating my growth,
watching even my eyeballs flutter.

Yet, those lifeless walls are
my only armour,
my only comfort,
my complete protection.

Stay Alert by Bill Lythgoe

Wake up
at the back.
Make sure you listen

To politicians
mouthing slogans
into your home.

We are relying
on the scientists
who are advising us.

Protect the community.
Keep on spreading
herd immunity.

Statistics assure us
the rate at which deaths
are increasing is decreasing.

If you don't break the rules,
schools are safe,
like care homes used to be.

Wash your hands
and free key workers
from virtual lockdown.

You can play tennis
but do not touch
your opponent's balls.

There's no cash at all
for the NHS
so remember to clap.

Download the app.
Don't ask why or how but wear
a mask if you have one.

Take care on the M1.
Avoid too many
Cummings and goings.

It's a no brainer.
We can beat the virus
like we beat the remainers.

Isolation by Bill Lythgoe

We hang out to dry
in the morning sunshine
of the warm spring garden.

We can barely hear
the background hum
of the M6 Motorway.

A pigeon croons
its love song, but today
gets no response.

Sam hammers a nail
into his fence and waves to us
from a safe distance

while the boys at number eight
seem almost afraid
to make a noise.

They whisper as if still sitting
in the back row
of a quiet classroom.

No footballs bounce across the street.
No ice cream vans
ring out their tunes.

Nothing to disturb the sleep
of old George next door
as he snores in his wheelchair.

The Old Courts by Mark Sixsmith

Windows by Reggie Doherty

It's That Time of Day Again
- Let's Eat
by Tara Lloyd

'Stay Alert'
said the sludge to the pigeon
by Tara Lloyd

48

20 Crumb Distance
by Tara Lloyd

We May Be Lonely But We
Can Be Lonely Together
by Tara Lloyd

49

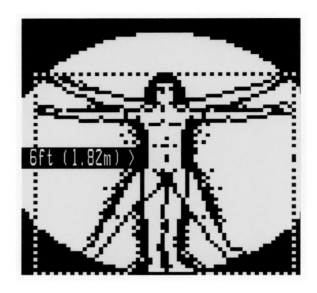

Virustruvian

The Carrier

Lockdown Hand

by Dan Farrimond

Melting Face

Stay Indoors

Lockdown Kit

by Dan Farrimond

51

Graduation at Home, June 2020 by Elizabeth-Anne Broad

16th June 2020 Mercedes Broad had virtual graduation at home in Skelmersdale having had to leave Kings College, University of Aberdeen on 22nd March 2020 and complete her studies online.

Dad in Work 1970s
by Elizabeth Anne Broad

Mercedes grandad, Tim Moran, spent 47 years working at the Crawford Street, 'Makerfield Magistrates Court'. Just as Mercedes had a mad dash home this March, Tim had escaped German invasion of Guernsey where he was at school. World War 2 meant that he didn't go to university and there was no graduation for him. Instead he served with the Royal Navy in Burma and the Far East. But it didn't stop him becoming a lawyer and Clerk to the Magistrates at the Old Courts until closure.

Why No Hugs? by Pete Coulson

A Clear Sky in Scholes, on a Once a Day Exercise
by Anna Croxhall

A Covid-19 Spring Day in Whelley II
by Anna Croxhall

Birthday Celebrations by Angela Halliday
The world of excitement and enjoyment through a child's eyes, not aware of what was approaching and that this would be the the last time that they would see each other again for a long time. It shows the innocence of children.

**Blurred Around the Edges
by Sue Lewis**

58

Doodle
by Johnny McGarr

59

**Endless
Home Deliveries**

**By
Brenda Brown**

Hand Sanitiser

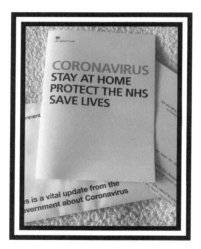

Stay at Home

Anti-body Test

Online Groceries

**Finding Joy in Nature
- The Best Things in Life
Are Free
by Tony France**

**Flower
by Mike Obern**

Image
by Paul Southward

June 2020
Bridge Over M6 Hardly
Any Traffic
by Susan Rigby

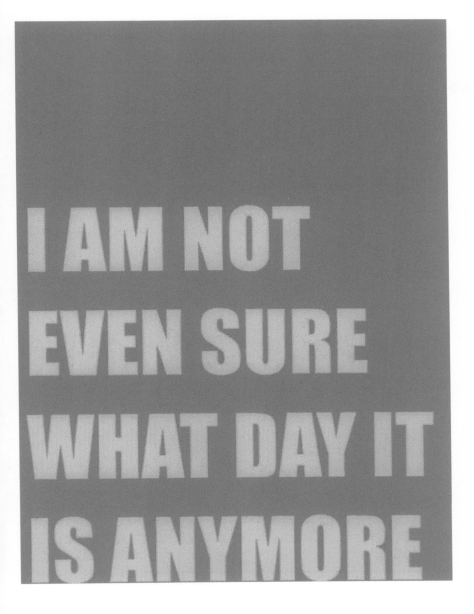

Lockdown Humour
by Charlotte Robinson

63

Summer Storm by Martin Holden

Mill
by Mike Obern

**Mary Jean Topping
by Tony Topping**

Park Locked World Locked
by Rhiann Such

Photo of Lockdown
by Gloria Green

**Quarantine by
Reece Mclean**

Skem Quarantine Grotto
How We Hoped for Better Days
by Helen Birnbaum

**The Naked Guitarist UK
by Stuart Hesketh**

The Three Heads, Pagefield Mill, Wigan
by Susan Rigby

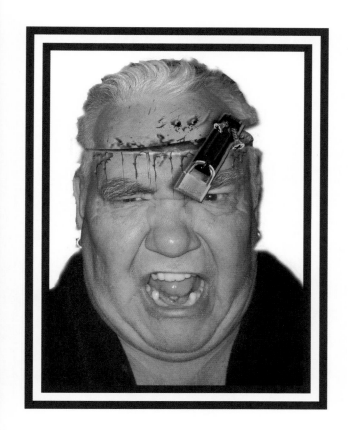

Unlocked by Peter Slater

VE Day 75 by Brenda Brown

Misunderstood by Elyse Dutton

Wigan Mail Office Delivery Support for the NHS by Jack Cooke

**Just a Memory
by Tara Lloyd**

Each day began to feel like the same. The same typical British weather. Isolated within our own walls. Looking through the same windows...this bright yellow children's toy remained to glow yellow each day within the garden.

Each Day Began to Feel the Same
by Charlotte Robinson

Sunflowers = Happiness by Edith Sass

World Corona Flat by Rachel Holmes

Inspired by the Covid 19 pandemic. I have illustrated the corona virus orbiting the earth.
It has got the whole world in it's grasp but we need to stay true
to our roots and true to one another in this hardship.
Keep safe, wash your hands.

No 73
by Louise Brandwood Price

Coronavirus
by Oliver Wood

In 2020 a pandemic was declared, but the news held so much uncertainty.
As large gatherings, holidays and events put on hold, it spread universally.
Asking has anyone travelled to or been to other countries had any of these symptoms?
As the coronavirus quickly spreads, we watch hopelessly as it claims its first victims.
The government announce that elderly, young and the sick are most vulnerable.
We worry for our loved ones, as other countries, a lockdown to be considerable.
Soon panic and bulk buying consumes and grips the nation, pasta, milk and toilet rolls.
Education, employment and the NHS struggles, we worry for their loss of roles.
Soon the government announce the pandemic and we have certain guidelines.
The symbol of a rainbow for hope for all the keyworkers fighting on the frontlines.
The coronavirus claims more victims, the government declares nationwide lockdown.
Masks, gloves and social distancing are declared, unessential shops close down.
No visiting, no large groups and home schooling, households have to stick together.
An hour exercise in your local area, social distance shopping, walks in all weather.
Day by day the news on the pandemic is still uncertain, as they seem to intertwine.
Excited to take out bins, clap on a Thursday, listen about hero's with lives on the line.
Worry taking over, people being named or blamed, stay home protect our keyworkers.
Hobbies restarted, gardening, cleaning and DIY, some turning into world class bakers.
Technology helps to stay in touch with families and friends, no news yet of a deadline.
The symbol of a rainbow for hope for all the keyworkers fighting on the frontlines.
In times of so much negativity, we had a veteran raising money and other heroic stories.
It gives me hope for humanity, we can look back on this pandemic in some form of glories.
That we stuck together and helped each other when needed, let's look at the positivity's.
Life is precious, time is precious, the planet is precious and time with more perceptivity.
That war and pain, just brings more war and pain, that these actions cannot be undone.
That money and our possessions cannot buy absolute happiness, when all said and done.
We need to be heroes; we need to protect our world and our lives will benefit in the long run.
So, I cannot wait for the pandemic to be over, to celebrate the keyworkers on the frontlines
The symbol of a rainbow for hope for all the keyworkers fighting to give people a lifeline.

My Story
by Paige Ellis-Forshaw (Aged 6)

Sadly, my school closed. I should've been in class 2G, instead I was waving goodbye to my fabulous friends.

When I heard the nasty news, I felt quite scared. The following day I started to think what would become of us. I had mixed emotions and slithering snakes in my tummy.

I thought the home schooling was wonderful because I got taught maths at the same time as being with my loving parents. It was a bit weird being taught by my mum and dad, but I got used to it in the end. Even mum and I had a naughty giggle during the lessons!

When I went outside, I learnt how to ride my beautiful bike (without stabilisers) for the first time! I Loved it and I was so pleased! Usually, I do not get much spare time to do this because I'm at school.

As I was missing my friends my mum kindly let me face time them (something I had never done before). That was fun!

I enjoyed the Lock-down. It was brilliant being able to spend lots of time doing new pastimes.

On Reflection by Millie Ellis-Forshaw (Aged 8)

When I arrived at school, I was told Friday would be the last day. At first I was shocked. My friends and I had a little celebration but at the same time we felt upset not knowing when we would play together again.

We went into lockdown. I felt sad because I wouldn't see my friends and teachers for a while yet thrilled because I could spend extra time with my family. I got to do lots more super, fun activities with them that I wouldn't normally have the chance to do. We played netball, rode our bikes around the garden and even went on a huge walk around the fresh, local fields and sweet, little village. My sister and I planted colourful seeds, baked scrumptious cakes with mum and we even learned how much fun it was to play Monopoly!

Even though it was amazing at home I was still concerned because I didn't want any of us going into isolation in hospital should we become ill. Also, My Aunty Colette was already poorly so I feared if she would catch the virus.

When we weren't being home schooled, we played for many hours in the glorious, spring sunshine and we splashed in the cool pool like cute, baby dolphins.
From all the washing of hands and Ambulance sirens I hope now even after the wonderful times, Covid19 clears up and goes away.

Covid-19 - Alone in Lockdown (Abridged)
by Shiela Lucas

Well, here we are then. Who'd have thought we'd ever be in a situation like this? I remember just as lockdown was starting I paid a visit to the doctor's surgery to collect a prescription. I wasn't allowed in and had to communicate with the receptionist over an intercom. She eventually passed it to me cautiously through a half opened door. Next door, the pharmacist was clad in mask and gloves. Standish had taken on an eerie atmosphere with no traffic and half empty shelves in the supermarkets. It was reminiscent of a scene from a science fiction film and I half expected to see armoured vehicles carrying men in white protective suits brandishing spray cannons of anti-bacteria to come rumbling down the high street. It felt unnatural and I was glad to get home.

A rush of confused thoughts still swirl through my head as I try to follow the news reports without screaming. Every time I turn on the TV the first words I hear are "Covid-19" and I know that programmes, news and even advertisements will be punctuated by it for the rest of the day. I do want to keep abreast of how the situation is progressing, but I'd like a little respite too.

My heart breaks for those who have fallen foul of this dreadful virus in any way, and it's right that we should know about them, but the constant long faces and funereal tones of the presenters are not good for morale. It's true that the situation is grave but a lot of the relentless media coverage is inflammatory, counterproductive and downright depressing.

It harps on about poor mental health without realising it probably contributes to half of it! Let's try to find a little positivity too before we all decide there's no use bothering with anything anymore.

And, yes the NHS workers are amazing and self-sacrificing and deserve recognition and gratitude, but so is my daughter who has worked all through this lockdown in a supermarket where customers don't seem to see the need for distancing. She doesn't have any PPE. Is she not just as heroic? Media hype is biased and only acknowledges other key workers almost as an afterthought.

Mistakes have been made too, but mistakes would have been made whoever was in power. This virus has presented us with a situation we have never experienced before. Wisdom is easy with hindsight and then everyone becomes an expert. I have no political affiliations and I think it will be time to pick over the bones of current strategies when the worst of this pandemic is over. Right now the powers that be need to work together. They can put on the boxing gloves later.

Right, enough ranting! I'm lucky. There I've said it. The main problem I have is that I'm widowed and live alone. Underlying health problems put me at risk and so I isolate conscientiously. However, I have lots of hobbies which are occupying me to the extent that I can't find time for housework. Tapping into my creative side is a joy. Singing, playing my ukulele and guitar and putting pen to paper, (sorry, finger to keyboard), is keeping the little grey cells functioning. Or so I thought until I found a roll of tin foil in the fridge. I hope I haven't put any food anywhere strange. Peculiar dreams have plagued my sleep too. One had me pouring a kettleful of boiling water into the toaster.

It seemed normal at the time. Another saw me chasing a delivery man down the street for playing "Tap latch" when delivering a parcel. Lockdown fever?

The big challenge with lockdown is to try to prevent each day being "Groundhog Day". A semblance of routine is good but not if it's followed slavishly. So a bit of this and that and phone and Facebook chats with different friends and chat is not just on a "loop". Not easy when nothing much happens. There was a pleasant interlude, though, when the street had a socially distanced party for VE Day. Everyone had picnics in the bunting bedecked front gardens, sang together and danced (six feet apart, of course) down the middle of the street. A good day.

So I set myself targets – learn or write a new song, write a sketch, invent a new recipe, rearrange the cupboards to name but a few. Am I lonely? Yes. Sometimes it feels less like self-isolation and more like solitary confinement.

I live a virtual life that keeps me safe and which caters for all my basic needs - except for the most important one. A hug.

The Queue 2020 by Tina Finch

Heavenly Rainbow
by Brandon Martin (Aged 6)

The Language of Lockdown by Gloria Green

A New Normal by Ellie Bolland

NHS National Health Superheroes
by Amelie Leggott (Aged 6)

New Arrival in Lockdown by Ron Wade

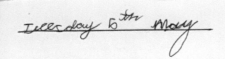

Tuesday 5th May

A story about a virus.

This is a story about a virus that started,

and all the people had to stay parted,

The world had a really big fight,

To make everything right,

we went on walks,

and had lots of talks,

some times we got sad,

which made us feel a bit mad,

but other times we felt happy,

because we thaut about seeing our

Grandparents, nanna and papa.

92

A Story About A Virus
by Amelie Leggott (Aged 6)

Help yourself to my homemade wine glass charms and
let's toast all the key workers.

Hope is in Kindness
by Jack Smith

**Herons Wharf
by Richard Benbow**

After the storm is rainbow

**Life in Lockdown
by Sara Lawlor**

95

**Lockdown Bear
by Clare Crossan**

Queue at Beech Hill
by Lora Marsden

I was waiting in a long queue down Gidlow lane in Wigan in order to collect my medications from the Pharmacy at Beech Hill Medical Practice. It was a moment I just couldn't shake. Not because it was particularly frightening or distressing, I just felt it really captured a lot of the uncertainty/tension that seemingly everyone was experiencing at that time despite what a lovely sunny day it was.

Social Distancing
by Sue Lewis

Painting by Sue Lewis

Lockdown Garden - Where Is My Family?
by Karen Thompson

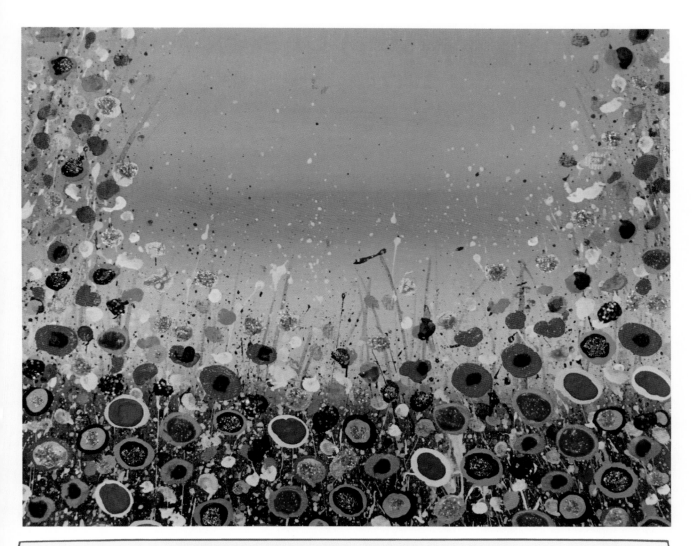

A New Beginning by Hazel Hobson

In these times of uncertainty and anxiety for many, nature will always provide a continuity of beauty, life and colour. Rest assured, times will change and it'll be Spring once more.

Happy 100th Birthday
Captain Tom

**Captain Tom's 100 Birthday
by Amelie Leggott (Aged 6)**

Sick 'Smiles' by Jenny Knowles

For my portrait, I would like to photograph my grandfather. Right now I, he and my family are going through a tough time with COVID-19. He is the glue of our family and I would like to photograph the struggle that he is facing and show everyone, including himself, how strong he really is. I wanted to use the natural lighting and shadows, to show the true feelings that are being kept inside compared to the ones being shown.

Grieving in Lockdown by Michelle Myers

Nan, you already lived in a world of confusion.
As dementia had you in its grip of delusion.
For 10 years, you battled that cruel disease.
And we were with you all the way, even if on our knees.
Then COVID19, reared its ugly head.
And the care home you lived, was locked up with dread.
Six long weeks went by, and we could not see you.
Then the phone call we feared, we prayed was not true.
Your health was failing, you were leaving this world.
But still COVID kept us apart no matter how my head whirled.
We had battled dementia together, we were with you every step of the way.
But COVID had other plans, for when it was your parting day.
My heart was broken. You had left this town.
Then began the process of grieving in lockdown.
Isolated, confused, separated and hurt.
New instructions from the government to stay alert.
But what about your funeral, the one that would be unjust.
The funeral directors promised it would be lovely if we trust.
And guess what, they were right. It was a beautiful day.
You had your home street lined, with people clapping away.
The cemetery was peaceful, with the sky above.
The birds were tweeting and friends gathered with love.
And I know you checked out, when the time was right.
For the pubs had closed and the world was at fight.
You're at peace now nan. Your work here is done.
Your memory will live on as we remember the fun.
Friends and family will plant the memorial seeds I made.
We will watch them grow with love as your tributes are paid.
I love you nan with all my heart.
Forever in my life you will remain the most influential part.
Your life was a blessing, you're at peace now so rest.
To me nan, you were undoubtedly simply the best.

Grieving in Lockdown by Michelle Myers

What They Make of Us by Jemima Longcake

On the television screen names flicker.
Names never uttered above hush-tones
anymore, we are immune to the suffering so we
don't scream.
There's pain in even the sound of hope, that we
collect,
and sometimes it's too real to face so we whisper
instead.
News of disease, air strikes, war and famine have
left us panicked and everything around us seems
so quiet now.

Except the birds.
I wonder what they make of us: our stories, and
words rolled into novels.
Our hopes, yes they exist, our panic too.
Our houses are dropped matchboxes on their
landscape.
Our way of life a fire starter and our way of
living we believe is harder than theirs, flying
over soil,
in joy bringing praise of life, and journey.
I wonder what they make of us; the birds.
I wonder what they make of silence in death,
because every night
I'm blessed with their singing.

Covid-19 Diary:
Extracts from Twelve Days Preceding and One Week into Lockdown (Abridged) by Catherine Holgate

Wednesday 11th March 2020

Today, Boris Johnson made another speech about the virus which was officially labelled a pandemic. It sounds very serious. He is probably pleased about it because the media frenzy is now directed away from the hash his government is making in Brussels.

On our dog walks, Sarah keeps talking about stocking up. Pete told her last week maybe she should buy "a few" extra cans. She says she has now stocked up. Unlike me, she watches the television news. I wonder if television media is really razzing things up.

Thursday 12th March

Stock markets worldwide suffer their greatest single-day fall since the 1987 crash in response to the coronavirus pandemic and the previous day's announcement of a 30-day travel ban between the U.S. Europe. No point in cashing in on those shares jointly owned by my mum and Aunt then! They asked me to look into this for them a week or so ago. I should have got my finger out. Pilates today. I take my own bands and mats as Kay has warned us she can't clean the ones she supplies satisfactorily. We have a laugh as usual, especially at Ken's antics. He's probably about seventy, thin, gangly, always grinning and friendly.

He used to be a colleague of Kay's mum, who also attends, so they know each other very well and there is a lot of banter. Most weeks there is a point where he struggles to follow multiple instructions to amusing effect and then he plays up to it when we laugh. He's good at hip-hinge squats, however, reaching perfect right angles so that he looks like he's sitting on an invisible, but uncomfortable chair.

Covid-19 Diary:
**Extracts from Twelve Days Preceding and One Week
into Lockdown (Abridged) by Catherine Holgate cont.**

Following that, I go to Tesco to stock up a little bit(!) Our cupboards are pretty empty – only a tin of chickpeas and a tin of kidney beans remaining. I was thinking about gradually boosting the store cupboard, but when I get to Tesco, people are being crazy. The first thing I notice is the sheer quantity of milk in people's trolleys. One woman has six three-litre bottles of milk on the conveyor belt and the bottom of a large trolley filled double depth with bottles of UHT milk.

In an effort to be non-judgmental, I surmise that perhaps she runs a guest house or café and is not a complete fruit-loop! Fresh fruit and vegetables are obviously not high priority as there are plenty. The pasta aisle is next. Only lasagne sheets are left. No-one intending to cook from scratch then. Perhaps it's the thought of making a cheese sauce! I am relieved to see the free-from aisle is still well stocked.

In home-baking, there is an absence of eggs and flour stocks are low. Next: tins and jars. Although the top (staff-only) shelf empty, there is still plenty on the customer shelves, so I get eight tins of tomatoes, six of baked beans, four soups and four tuna. I need UHT milk for Harvey's yogurt making and just in case. There is not one bottle left. And as for toilet roll, the entire length of one side of a massive (10-15m long) aisle is dedicated to toilet roll in Wigan Tesco Extra.

Not a chance – all gone!

Monday 23rd March

I have discussed the home schooling with Anais. I have given her choices about when and how much work she does. We are agreed that she will get the school exercises out of the way in the morning, then we can do fun, educational activities in the afternoon. She does Reading Plus, three Times Tables Rock Stars sound checks and a comprehension sheet from the file. In the afternoon, we attack the compost heap and use the compost to plant some seeds (sunflower, parsley, violets, little red flowers – I forget the name). I can't buy new seed, and our seeds are all out of date, so it will be interesting to see if any germinate!

There are thousands of worms in the compost heap. We look up online how to make a wormery and then make one, using some of the worms from the compost heap

Wednesday 25th March

Anais does not manage to get up during their self-isolation. My phone pings constantly with messages and funny videos, from the various WhatsApp groups I'm a member of, about life in lockdown: a man in a tight, women's gymnastics leotard demonstrating a dance with hilarious names for the dance moves; a child who is stricken by grief because Nando's, McDonalds, KFC and all the Chinese restaurants are shut and she's going to have to eat food cooked by her mum; a Scouser films his groceries while he tells us how he went to the supermarket and the shelves were stripped bare, but when he went outside, he saw people with full shopping trollies and politely asked them if they would give him stuff.

This constant contact throughout the day is very comforting, funny and informative. My heart goes out to people working in the NHS. Karen R, a nurse in my uni friends group, told us that they were "... in an all-day meeting... being shown how to properly put on protective equipment (the thinnest plastic aprons money can buy & masks that cause you to cough!)...". She's convinced she will catch the virus, and I have to say, so am I.

I realise I've got a cushy job here. As frustrating as it is trying to find time to write my diary, prepare for my historical blog and keep up the creative writing amongst all the home-schooling, housework, and 'social work' with all the old folks I need to keep an eye on, it's an oasis compared with the horror of working in the NHS.all the work set by school done today.

I write her a series of questions about it on the computer and she answers them and goes online to research the animals we found in the compost heap and to cut and paste pictures of them.

Through the day, I make time to message Andrew, Sue, Majda, my uni friends, the year 4 mums' group, call Maralyn, FaceTime Averil, and make three calls to Mum to check all are okay and keep them buoyed up during their self isolation.

My phone pings constantly with messages and funny videos, from the various WhatsApp groups I'm a member of, about life in lockdown: a man in a tight, women's gymnastics leotard demonstrating a dance with hilarious names for the dance moves; a child who is stricken by grief because Nando's, McDonalds, KFC and all the Chinese restaurants are shut and she's going to have to eat food cooked by her mum

2020 - The Year Coronavirus Spread Over the World by Pauline Bradley (Aged 82)

At the beginning of the year, I said to my elder daughter,

'I have a good feeling about this year.'

She replied,

'Oh good Mum, I know you have a strong intuition about people and places.' So we began with lots of hope that this year would bring changes and good times.

Well, nearly 3 months on, my intuition has taken a battering – don't think anyone would have anticipated the change that has come about with this deadly coronavirus, not just in this country, but every country in the world.

When news began to filter through about a disease from Wuhan in China, probably we had all thought it would be contained in the East as in the past, but when queues began getting longer in the supermarkets like it was Christmas; and there was a rush to buy toilet rolls of all things, it started to look more serious.

Suddenly we were getting government bulletins every day this was a pandemic and we should all be staying at home to stop the NHS getting overwhelmed by a rush of patients suffering with this virus. This was serious, we had to batten down the hatches.

First I realised this was serious when my son-in-law text me to say everyone over 70yrs of age had to stay in for 3 months. 3 months?! I couldn't stay in that long. I live on my own and going out every couple of days was necessary to make me feel part of the human race still. But if I had to adapt, I would, so armed with new technology now to buy groceries online, taught by said son-in-law, I started my self isolating period. I was worried about getting my monthly prescription, but within a couple of days, a young man came to the door with an extra months supply, a nice surprise.

It was challenging, scanning and scrolling (new word!) the shopping menus, felt I had to rush it or it would disappear into thin air! With help from my younger daughter, I learnt what some of the symbols meant, still missed things though, didn't realise I could buy my newspaper & magazine online until she showed me the search symbol; easy when you know how, Oh Joy! – I could buy a paper!

2020 - The Year Coronavirus Spread Over the World
by Pauline Bradley cont.

Then another mystery, had to pick a delivery slot.. 'oh, what do you mean, I can't have it delivered same day?' After 9 weeks in, I think I've sorted it (well, I am 82!) but I'm sure there'll be something I've missed. On the plus side, don't need to buy petrol for the car or the dreaded job of putting air in the tyres!

I've missed not having the 2 grandsons coming in the house and only seeing them through the window, not able to hug them or go and see them in their house just down the road. Very strange.

My elder grandson wasn't bothered about missing school for a few weeks, but after 2 months is missing seeing his friends. His mum has kept them busy, baking, learning Spanish, having cycle rides where allowed, having a pool in the garden when its been hot. My elder daughter who lives in Devon has kept me and my disabled sister (also in her eighties) busy remembering our childhood, places we lived, went to school and how the areas have changed over eighty years, we have fun finding out about our ancestors, where they lived, what they did with our lives. This project certainly helped with our isolation and filled the days with our virtual company.

Also enjoyed the garden, sowing seeds etc in a small plastic greenhouse, watching them develop into fine, young plants. Growing strawberry plants sent from Devon to plant into a planter bought as a Christmas present.

It is an odd sensation knowing that millions of people across the World are doing the same as me, more or less at the same time. The World has certainly shrunk.

I wonder if this unusual time has brought people closer to each other from different countries; we are not so much different, even if we speak in different languages and have other cultures. Basically we want the same things from life; to be loved, to be happy, to have enough food, to survive and be a member of a family.

It must be a challenge to young people especially with young children to get through this. They will remember it for the rest of their lives, like the older generation remember the War years, which went on for 6 years.

Maybe the good feeling I had at the beginning of the year wasn't what I expected, but it has turned out very differently to what we all thought it would be, that we can't take anything for granted.

112

Isolation Poem
by Dominic Smith (Aged 8)

Running around to keep fit
All playing a part to help
Isolating to save others
NHS working hard to save lives
Being away from family
One day more home schooling
We came back together

**Wallgate When Lockdown Began
by Susan Rigby**

**Wigan Pier Walks With Finn
by Susan Rigby**

Half Full
by Peter Aspinall

Half Full.
Cirrus clouds skulk off as the sun spews rays.
Soon citizens sickly from the several ciders they supped yesterday will slither slowly out of their slumber.
Heads spinning. Sobering up slowly.
Safe in the knowledge that today will be just as hatefully similar as yesterday and sure that tomorrow will be the same.
Seems like a subdued Saturday every day these days, it's strikingly surreal.
Still, the street survives.
Surprising, since shockingly some subjects seem to think sunshine somehow releases them from lockdown. They assemble, they swarm. They sit. Stupidly, side by side. I resist, I struggle, I stem the compulsion to issue forth a shot of verbal venom. The stress!
Stress.
The silent sorrow spawned by my sufferance of these selfish simpletons and my irritating incongruence as I smile and send salutations as I saunter down the street.

The anger, the annoyance these people elicit in me is enough to give me dyspepsia!
Smile, saunter, salutations.
The strain is only eased by the assumption of a sliver of assurance that this shall surely pass sometime.
Delusional dunce or hopeful halfwit?
It doesn't matter, stay sanguine.
Slowly, imperceptibly so, it starts to seem surprisingly sunny.
Cider might suffice.
But only half a glass. Honest.
Sat in a swimming pool in the garden.
Soaking up the Sun.
It's the only sensible way to survive these strange days.
With a scintillating sense of optimism, and a glass half full.

Half Full by Peter Aspinall

22 March 2020 by Josie Byrne

I shopped happily in a store,
checked in my diary
to see if I had a window.
On the day before.

I made plans for a weekend away,
welcomed with joy a bright sunny day.
Pushed how far I could go,
On the day before.

I did a journey on a train,
recoiled in horror as a man coughed,
and coughed again,
I was so glad when he got off.
On the day before.

I looked in horror at my hair,
need a hairdresser,
So badly need to go there.
On the day before.

22 March 2020 by Josie Byrne cont.

I went out with friends to see a show,
then had a lovely meal.
the conversation,
it just flowed
Oh and the wine tasted fine.
On the day before.

When I came home
I switched on the tv
Oh Em Gee!
How had this come to be?
My heart started to ache
and become sore,
On the day before.

I slept poorly,
Surely this was just a bad dream,
It cannot be as bad as it seems.
I walked the floor
On the day before.

31 Thousand Thoughts and Counting
by Shaun Fallows

All information
Was inflammation
Arriving later than a British Rail train
31 thousand thoughts
and counting left to bathe in r own brain
Don't dare pass that off as part victory
Any hope was hiding in our homes
The search party
Was now a watch party
With out of the blue, lost friend calls
We could noisy at house decorating on the walls
Any hope was hiding in our homes
& To be Frank Anne we needed it
Cos braking bad
beneath all this
Are proper people
The sleeps stopping

Until
I've got claustrophobic ceilings
Messed up mind of matrix feelings
The reality that could never be reality
The body dysmorphic fear
That made me sick
Any time I didn't want to hear
Is shouting again
Shouting in my face
With those 31 thousand thoughts and counting

Adjustment by Dawn Marie Baxter

The virus arrives
As our life rearranges

The virus takes over
As our life changes

The virus takes precious lives
As our life deranges

The virus takes its toll
As our life disengages

The virus is subsiding
As our life moves back in stages

The virus will make us stronger
As our life rewrites the pages.

A Thousand Drops by Catherine West-McGrath

I felt another drop of kindness
Fall on my gate today
Leaving behind the bread and apples
Asking 'Are you okay?'

(Chorus)
And who knows what we leave behind us?
A thousand drops of love and kindness
And who knows what we'll leave behind today?

You travelled over a thousand miles
To be there at his side
To watch him as he fell asleep
And afterwards we cried

I felt another drop of kindness
Fall in my hands today
Leaving behind a children's rainbow
Asking 'Are you okay?'

(Chorus)

You travelled over a thousand door steps
To let me know you cared
I heard applause fill up the sky
On evenings that we shared

I felt another drop of kindness
Fall on my eyes today
Leaving behind a wave through windows
Asking 'Are you okay?'

(Chorus)

You travelled over a thousand notes
To let us share your stage
To play some music for my soul
Tell stories from your page

I felt another drop of kindness
Fall in my heart today
Leaving behind a hopeful future
Asking 'Are you okay?'

(Chorus)

Be Kind Be a Friend by Terry Burtonwood

Covid 19 we're all under attack
I'm ok the wife's "got my back."
Imagine that you're living on your own
That there's only you in your home.

It must be purgatory with nobody there
Feeling isolated, sat, in the same old chair
Prisoners in solitary; is the hardest thing they do
Yet this is what's happening to you.

No ones coming to your door
Posts the only thing landing on your floor
You haven't spoken to anyone for weeks
Television that's your only treat

TV doesn't always help, death toll details
Enough to send you off the rails
Weeks progress, you talk to the voice in your head
Sometimes you think you'd be better off dead.

So come on people don't leave them alone
Do the right thing pick up the phone
Care workers stopped going, they're scared to death
Come on they'd welcome anyone on their step.

So make the effort be kind and make someone's day
Always remember to stay two metres away
They haven't spoken to anyone for weeks on end
Show them you care, just be a good friend.

Boo by Tafara Burrows (Aged 9)

She didn't like it at all when her father had to go down to London and, for the first time, she had to sleep alone in the old house.

She went up to her bedroom early. She turned the key and locked the door. She latched the windows and drew the curtains. She peered inside her wardrobe, and pulled open the bottom drawer of her chest-of-drawers; she got down on her knees and looked under her bed.

She undressed; she put on her nightdress.
She pulled back the heavy linen cover and climbed into bed. Not to read but try to sleep-she wanted to sleep as soon as she could. She reached out and turned off the lamp.
The telephone rang. The hoarse voice said "I'm watching you," ... and then the line went dead.

Suddenly, she felt a chilling hand touch he Surprise! To her astonishment her dad was bac She felt relieved that her dad was back an wasn't scared anymore. As she closed her ey(she thought "then who was that?" She was ju happy her dad was back. Or was he?

Almost immediately the next day came and sh was determined to find out who did the hoars voice and pranked her.

Her suspects where her dad and the neighbou the clues she had was the voice stopped whe dad came home. Determined to find an answe she efficiently checked the suspect's pockets t find nothing. She also asked questions to th suspect's to find out that dad was on his phon when it happened. So who was it?

In the Trenches (Abridged) by Steven Clarke

SCENE 1

FADE IN:

INT. A SMALL LIVING ROOM.

DE PROFILE. We open up on a squinting old man attempting to dial someone on his tablet. His fingers ake involuntary as he touches the dialling keypad on the screen. He is white and frail-looking from the little that we can see of him. His nose is almost touching the screen. The call is answered.

CUT TO: A close up of the tablet's display. All we can see is the interior of the old man's nostrils

FEMALE VOICE (OFF CAMERA)
Hello?

OLD MAN
'Ello? Margaret?

FEMALE VOICE
I'm sorry, but I can't see your face. Can you move away from the camera a bit?

THE OLD MAN PULLS AWAY FROM THE SCREEN REVEALING HIS FACE
FOR THE FIRST TIME. CUT TO HIS POV: WE SEE A SMILING YOUNG ASIAN WOMAN IN HER
MID-TO-LATE TWENTIES.

OLD MAN
Margaret, is that you?

YOUNG WOMAN
Sorry, I think you've got the wrong number. My name's Nina.

125

OLD MAN
Oh, I'm sorry, my love. I'm trying to call me daughter, but I can't see these bloody numbers
properly.

NINA (GIGGLING)
It's no trouble. Are you alright?

OLD MAN
Yes, dear, although, me bins are broken.

NINA (CONFUSED)
Your bins?

CUT TO: NINA'S POV

OLD MAN
Yeah, me bins. I remember I 'ad'em on to read the paper. I was reading about how Prince Charlie
got this flu thing what's going around, and I must have fallen asleep. Well, when I came to, they
weren't on me face anymore. So, I gets up to try and find 'em when I 'ears this almighty crack. I've
only gone and bloody stood on 'em.

NINA (GIGGLING)
Ohhh, you mean your glasses?! You really lost me there for a minute. What's your name, Sir?

OLD MAN
Stanley, dear. Stanley Cartwright.

NINA
Lovely to meet you, Stanley Cartwright.

126

It Feels Anything Less Like a Saturday - (Lockdown 2020)
by Brenda Brown

How do we even know these days, what day of the week it is, how many weeks we've been locked away in isolation …. a surreal prison sentence with nothing to distinguish the days other than maybe a weekly TV programme or a fleeting glance at the calendar. No! Have I really missed another Birthday? I'll have to send yet another message with a belated greeting.

I'm one of those 'of a certain age' that is considered more vulnerable. Am I? I haven't got any underlying health problems (that I know of) and yet I've been made to feel unfit and aged almost overnight. It isn't that long ago I was flying halfway across the world on another exciting adventure, feeling young and vibrant and challenged in a very positive way.

Now look at me – gorging my way through another box of chocolates, grazing and nibbling night and day to break through the boredom. There's no motivation to lose that stone in weight I've put on, having nowhere to go and having no-one visit. It's perhaps as well, given it's been 3 months without a hair cut and the beautiful gel nails that everyone once admired have long since gone.

Family – I so miss seeing them, especially the grandchildren. Those smiles and cuddles seem a million miles away now. I can only worry about them from a distance and hope they're safe and well. Human contact of any sort is something we so often take for granted – until we're not allowed it. Now we feel bereft. Those warm hugs, smiles and affectionate kisses are becoming only memories. Physical touch – a thing of the past.

I feel so lucky and privileged to have a garden in which I can sit and potter around. We have been blessed with mainly good weather during lockdown. Lucky for me and others similarly fortunate. I try to imagine how difficult it must be for those locked away in high rise flats or other gardenless properties, the sun beating down outside, unable to escape except for the obligatory short walk to the park, or more recently a short drive to a beauty spot or the beach, remembering of course to return the same day ... unless of course your name is Dominic Cummings!

Sitting in the garden reading a book, or just sitting in the sun, I notice more clearly this year the blossoms that are in abundance during April and May. The deep purple droplets of the wisteria hang like opulent grapes from a vine. One of the most quintessential of English garden plants, it's my pride and joy. It has often been greatly admired, but this year I must enjoy its beauty alone. Keeping it company are the azaleas and clematis with their varied and vibrant colours.

I have seen them all bud, blossom and fade during lockdown. But the roses have now appeared, and if they don't get blown away by the violent winds we have been experiencing they will now take centre stage in the Coronavirus garden.

Of late, I've tried to take a short walk every day avoiding the main roads of course in case I bump into someone coming the other way forcing me to sidestep into the path of oncoming traffic. I walk around housing estates instead, seeing people only occasionally and with room to manoeuvre. As I walk, I admire people's lockdown endeavours – cars that are clean and shiny, beautifully waxed and polished (unlike mine), lawns that are mown within an inch of their lives, pristine garden layouts, newly painted fences and walls. In one garden, all pots have been newly painted to match their surroundings – must have got a job lot of paint from B&Q! The scene reminds me of gardens I would see on a trip to the seaside as a child glistening in the sunshine and screaming 'look at me – I'm different than your normal suburbia', sitting among equally bright and happy garden gnomes, windmills and garishly coloured wind spinners.

It Feels Anything Less Like a Saturday - (Lockdown 2020) by Brenda Brown cont.

Some days I'm lazy, or forgetful - or both. I don't go for a walk and instead watch tv, read a book or try to endure in my own garden in an attempt to make it look anywhere near as pristine and cared for as the ones I see on my short travels. One thing that is consistent, whether indoors or out, is the troubling sound, day and night, of ambulance sirens which I imagine are carrying to hospital yet another victim of this terrible virus. I say a little prayer that whoever it is, they will survive.

Note, housework isn't among the things top of the list if I'm indoors. As to that, I have become, not surprisingly, unmotivated. I see the dust piling up and the crumbs on the floor, but it takes extreme effort to get out the dust cloth or the hoover. A bit like the hair and the nails – who's around to see them except me!

Then there was VE Day. It was amazing to see how people attempted to mirror the stoicism of that which had been celebrated 75 years ago. Many streets were dressed in bunting and flags.

It had been made a Bank Holiday to enable street parties and other celebrations to take place but sadly the planning was well before lockdown. On the day itself, I saw blokes dressed in World War II army uniforms and ladies with headscarves and 'pinnies', mimicking those worn in the 1940s. I heard talk of fabulous street parties, each household sitting in their own front gardens, still safe distancing. The weather was beautiful. There was no party in our street. I did put up the bunting and the flags, but they were only to be admired by the postman and the convoy of couriers delivering the constant flow of on-line shopping.

It Feels Anything Less Like a Saturday - (Lockdown 2020) by Brenda Brown cont.

Am I eating well? My waistline says too well. I feel guilty as I say that, thinking about all of those who have lost their jobs during this pandemic and are struggling to feed their families, relying on the kindness of others, food banks and charity. At first it was difficult to get hold of fresh produce (as well as loo roles, pasta, hand sanitiser, etc) but such things have now become more readily available. However, trying to book a home delivery slot with a local supermarket is nigh on impossible. Luckily, I have family who regularly visit Asda for either click and collect versions of on-line shopping or in store by queuing for up to two hours in the car park just to get in. I am eternally grateful for their enduring support.

Minimising the boredom? I would not survive without the fun and banter shared with family and friends via the miracle of Whatsapp – my only concession to social media. I don't do Facebook, TikTok, Twitter or anything else. The jokes, the photos, the funny and often irreverent videos have all helped to preserve my sanity and have enabled us all to laugh during this the most difficult of times.

I look forward every day to the messages which one family member in particular sends me – photographs from last year's holidays (look where we were this time last year!), depressing on the one hand (when will be ever be able to travel again?) but cheery on the other. Lovely memories and humorous episodes mixed with a longing that one day we might make more.

Fear and anxiety have certainly grown the longer we've been locked away. I'm not the only one affected; I talk to family – even the youngest member who, with no schools open and no friends to see, has lost so much. The social interaction they crave and need at that age has been snatched away from them.

It Feels Anything Less Like a Saturday - (Lockdown 2020) by Brenda Brown cont.

Who knows what will be the long-term damage to our health and wellbeing, mental health, education and the futures of a whole generation of learners and workers? It's like we're living in the middle of a Sci-Fi movie, but we don't seem any closer to knowing how it ends. Young people have depended even more than usual on social media, the internet and mobile phones (we all have). Within a variety of media, which on the one hand has brought much comfort and solace during these difficult times, there is also a dark side we must never forget. Bullying, domestic abuse and other forms of inconsiderate and harmful behaviour uncomfortably parallel the vast amount of warmth and human kindness the likes of which we have seen so much in recent months.

Clapping has become a weekly occurrence to show love and appreciation for our phenomenal NHS and other vital key workers. Every Thursday night I open my front door to hear the noise of clapping, spoons being bashed against pan lids, church bells and even, occasionally, fireworks. I rarely see anyone – I'm not facing another house, but I can hear the community spirit echoing around the street. I wonder if this spirit will remain once the pandemic is over. Will it ever be over? I sometimes sit here, lonelier and more isolated as the weeks go by and try to imagine a life the other side of lockdown.

May love, good health and happiness prevail.

Land of Confusion by Stephen Gall

We're all living in a land of confusion
Or is it all just a land of illusion
We're not allowed out except to go shopping
Not even on our relatives can we drop in
We're all doing online quizzes and reading loads of books
Making pies and puddings, we're all turning into cooks
Getting out old board games and doing jigsaws
Posting photo's of wildlife, Magpies and Jackdaws

I've been recording songs and poems, sharing them on Facebook
To several different Folk Club sites, anyone can take a look
These things I've been doing whilst I've been stuck in my flat
Eating all sorts of rubbish food, I think I might be getting fat
Thinking about what's caused all this, I'm a little less than cheery
I've not had a drink for two months, so it's not that I'm all beery
I've a theory about what's happened and what this is I'll tell
I think I must have died in March and of course I'm now in Hell

133

Let's be Kind Safe aand Fabulous by Chrys Ritson

Let's Be Kind, Safe and Fabulous
by Chrys Ritson

Well... The Bridge food bank didn't need me as a volunteer driver. The only elderly (and possibly diabetic) neighbour, for whom I offered to shop, only wanted me to buy her the blocks of chocolate that her daughter refused to put on the shopping list. I wanted to help my community in some small way but needed some creative ideas. All I could do was to get up each morning, a gesture that was starting to seem pointless, and take my small dog for a walk and a sniff round the fields and canal paths near where I live.

I live in a small Victorian terraced house with a back yard. There used to be a wash-house and when I had the slate roof removed from it, and replaced with Perspex, I kept the old slates. I knew eventually there would be a reason for hoarding them for twenty years.
It was on one of our morning dog walking ambles that a thought occurred to me. Not an original thought, just a reminder of something I had once read somewhere.

Be the person your dog thinks you are.

What kind of person does Luna think I am? Organised and energetic? I am neither of these things but my dog gets a regular walk and her food appears at set times, so my dog possibly thinks I'm both of these things. I wanted to be reminded to live up to be the person Luna thinks I am, so I painted the slogan onto one of the slates and hung it in a tree on my regular dog walking route.

She also possibly thinks I am sociable and creative. She is a black dog, and becomes invisible on our late night pre-sleep toilet walks unless she is bedecked in solar fairy lights. It makes sense to me and she submits to looking like a shaggy Christmas decoration. I think creative. Other folks might say eccentric. But at least I can see where she is.
There were many socially distancing dog walkers in Higher Green and, from a distance I noticed people stopping to read the sign.

So..... I painted another.

134

Help someone. You might be the only one who does.

I was still internally battling with the moral conundrum of should I buy chocolate for an elderly diabetic or was it patronising for me to decide that she shouldn't have it? Which was helping her? I wasn't happy with my decision, but decided that at 80 she was old enough to make her own choices and I bought the chocolate.

But the slate sign in the tree kept prompting me round that moral maze. I didn't know the answer, so perhaps the answer was to replace the painted slate with something that wasn't going to make me think.

Don't ever save anything for a special occasion. Being alive is the special occasion.

Well ... that didn't work either. It got me thinking about what I was saving for special occasions. Since the whole country had been told to stay home and not visit family or friends, or have them visit us – my standards of attire had slipped.

Gone were the bright summer clothes, the colourful scarves and gorgeous sun hats. Although the weather was glorious, it had become easier to pull on the leggings and a sloppy sweat shirt for the daily poo picking up. I was saving all my frivolous summer finery for post lock-down holidays .. and it looked like those weren't going to happen. So why not dress up and stay at home? So I did.

To celebrate the colourful butterfly emerging from the practical and dowdy chrysalis, I scrubbed a slate, painted it and hung it in a tree.

Let's Be Kind, Safe and Fabulous
by Chrys Ritson cont.

Be Kind, Safe and Fabulous.

Our socially isolated Crafty Friday group got involved too – thanks to the technical wizardry that is ZOOM and finding another stash of abandoned old roofing slates. We'd meet up at our various kitchen tables , gardens, conservatories and sewing rooms round the Borough and paint positive messages onto our slates whilst ZOOM chatting. We experimented with a range of media – acrylics, nail varnish, indoor and outdoor emulsion and, my particular favourite, masonry paint. I knew I'd kept that old tin, with an inch of paint in the bottom , for a reason. This was obviously the reason.

Suddenly positive slates, embellished with colourful and creative rainbows, flowers, stars, moons and fireworks, were hanging from trees in Lilford Woods and left anonymously in gardens to help raise energy and a fleeting smile.

Make the most of this day! Laugh. Love. Read. Live. Love!

Wherever you are …. be there.

Peace starts with a smile. (For VE day)

Enjoy Every Moment.

Rest now. Breathe easy and settle here where you are. We'll not move upon you for a while.

We are each unique and beautiful – just like buttercups.

Do something today that your future self will thank you for.

As I wafted round the lanes and tracks near my home in outrageous balloon trousers and pashminas, I became very aware that I was not the only one putting energy into making the best of how we look. The hawthorn bushes were covered tip to root in white blossoms, old apple trees looked young again in their pink and white froth. The football field, not having been mown by Wigan MBC ,was awash with dandilions buttercups, daisies and beautiful little blue flowers.

So I wrote part of a poem by Henrich Heine on a slate, to remind all my fellow dog walkers to lift their eyes from the reason they were carrying little poo bags and notice the beauty that was around them.

Let's Be Kind, Safe and Fabulous
by Chrys Ritson cont.

Sweet May has come to love us
Flowers, trees their blossoms don
And through the blue heavens above us
The very clouds move on.

During this period of lock-down I have taken time to get to know my neighbours a little more. Especially when we all came to our gates on Thursday evenings to clap in gratitude for the NHS. I have lived in my street for 35 years, but had never had a proper conversation with an elderly gentleman who, at the first rays of sunshine, sits of a chair by his front door to gave passers by a cheery wave.

One of the slates I painted was so appropriate for this gentleman that I took it off the tree and gave it to him. He has hung it on his fence.
How fine to watch the white clouds drift by.
I am sad for those who do not have the skill to sit still and do nothing.
Even sparrows know how to do this.

It is strange that I have had some tender and intimate conversations with strangers as we stroll two metres apart, while our dogs roll in muck without a care in the world. One lady shared her feelings of grief and sadness about not being able to be with her terminally ill dad. I obviously couldn't hold her hand, offer a hug or even a tissue as she wept her loss and grief. This is a cruel disease that takes people before their time. I don't know her name and all I could offer was a painted slate with a traditional Irish blessing.

Deep peace of the running wave to you.
Deep peace of the flowing air to you.
Deep peace of the quiet earth to you.
Deep peace of the shining stars to you.

This virus has reminded me that I am vulnerable and I should do as much as I can to stay healthy. I have painted some Tibetian advice on a slate and have hung it in my own yard to remind me of the wisdom of those monks in the mountains.
The secret to living well and longer is to eat half and walk double.
Easier written than done – no matter how many flowers and rainbows I paint on the slate.
Not all my slates have been profound and positive. Some have just recorded how I was feeling on that particular day.
I had plans to achieve amazing things during lock-down. But today I'm satisfied if I can eat a meal without getting food on my boobs.
And

I don't care what anyone thinks of me. Except dogs. I want dogs to like me.
I have no doubt that not everyone likes my painted slates. But, fortunately, I am now of the age when I don't care if I am written off as a mad old hippie. It's better than being ignored. One of my slates records an ancient Chinese proverb which reminds me to be myself-

The crooked tree lives a peaceful
life while the straight one end in planks.
We are all coping in our own ways with the situation in
which we find ourselves – and no one can predict how long we should isolate,
queue in supermarkets and wash our hands.
But as one of my Crafty Friday
friends painted on a slate
This is not the end of the story.
(and we still have
plenty of slates left!)

Let's Be Kind, Safe and Fabulous
by Chrys Ritson cont.

Post Script.

Like so many other people throughout the world I am saddened, shocked and horrified by the brutal murder, in broad daylight, of an George Floyd and all the other people who have suffered from injustice and inequality. I wanted to show my support and condemnation of such brutal racism, but what can one privileged, safe, middle-aged white woman in north west England do?.... apart from write on a slate a phrase suggested by my brother-in-law. So, as my tiny contribution to acknowledge and celebrate that Black Lives Matter – this will hang on a tree, not like a lynching, but as a phrase to which we can ALL aspire.
When the power of love overcomes the love of power the world will be at peace.

What Lockdown?
by Anne Sheila Livesey

What Lockdown?
I haven't noticed the difference – except the roads are quiet I believe
I can hear the birds sing loudly in the morning and evening and when I put their birdseed out
No kids knocking a ball against my garage, windows or door, but the sound of occasional drilling
and mowing but that happened anyway,
Before the lockdown I was alone
I never saw anyone
Never went out for drinks
Or walks
Or spoke to anyone on the phone
Never organised holidays in staycation or abroad with any bubble of friends
So
What's the difference?
My home is my sanctuary
Disease free
Toilets available so I don't disrespect the countryside or beach
I don't get drunk so don't miss the booze
I don't gossip so don't miss the goss
I'm used to repeats of TV
And don't watch or listen to any soaps so won't recognise the artificial worlds they cannot
portray

What Lockdown?
by Anne Sheila Livesey cont.

I don't watch the government broadcasts as I don't believe what they say anymore
Ever since I found out they do not do what they tell the rest of us to do.
I had little money before the lockdown so won't miss not having any
So what's the difference for people who live alone and already on low income?
My health ensured I can have home deliveries that's one good thing – but I have to leave it every
three weeks to afford the minimum purchase. I will continue to have the shopping delivered no
sense in putting myself in harms way, I used to go out very early in the morning but I do not
want to go on buses anymore.
See you one day, if you've got time to call, People across the road have never social distanced
from day one – they had visitors from different households every week.
Ah well,
Let me get back to UK Gold
LONELY PERSON

Lockdown Blues
by Brian Ratcliffe

Everyday's Sunday running on a loop,
Feel like a chicken locked up in a coop.
Same old same old is the name of the game,
Familiar routine's becoming quite tame.
Not much to smile about, brings on a frown,
Lockdown experience's dragging me down.

Losing It In Lockdown
by Brian Ratcliffe

I catch myself in the mirror
And soon decide : enough's enough.
I cannot get to the barbers.
I'm looking like a total scruff.

There's only one solution now,
Do some thinking outside the box.
So I become the barber and
DIY my disheveled locks.

And now that all the white hair's gone
I'm like a massive snooker ball.
Do I resemble a Zen monk?
Could be a convict after all.

Guard of Honour
by Brian Ratcliffe

Those heroes dressed in PPE
Took some time out so they could see
The people they had helped restore
Now heading for the exit door.
They wheeled them through the corridors
A guard of honour gave applause.
The smiling faces show relief,
Though there remains a sense of grief
For those who paid a heavy cost
As we still mourn the ones we lost.

Why No Hugs?
by Pete Coulson

Why no hugs?

I've seen them in Mesnes Park a few times now. I call them the little shy family. They all stay close together and the children don't seem to want to play as you'd expect them to. The little boy clings to his toy very tightly, I notice, even though it's getting a bit tatty.

I suppose I'm more aware of people at the moment. It's partly my age and my slow, trundling pace. And it's partly the lockdown dance we're all doing. Do you know what I mean? It's when you see someone coming and you move to one side of the path, they move to the other side, you catch their eye and you both smile. I call that the lockdown dance.

I like the smile especially, like we really are all in this together, except that Dominic Cummings of course. We're not used to smiling at strangers when we go round Wigan. When Harry was alive we'd say hello to people at the top of the Plantations near Haigh Hall but then the nearer you got to town walking back, the more you'd feel you had to get back to normal and walk straight past.

Not past people you knew, of course, and there's always plenty of them every time you turn out. That's one thing about living here all your life.

The little shy family don't look as if they've been here all their lives. Not very long at all, I imagine. I don't know why they caught my interest really. Call me nosy if you like but the little girl reminds me of you when you were a toddler, Julie. I can imagine her with that red cherry bobble in her dark hair. You know, I saved that for years. I may even have it somewhere still, tucked away in that old cardboard box at the back of the bottom drawer.
I wonder …

Do you remember reaching up to post bits of stale bread through the round bits of the railings by the duck pond? Well, that's where they were when I first saw them. The children seemed pleased when I smiled.

I heard on the radio you're not supposed to feed bread to ducks now, but we didn't know any better in those days. So much has changed, hasn't it love? Nowadays it's not even a shock to see a young family with brown skin in Mesnes Park. I like it though. It feels like we're connected to the rest of the world. Mrs Johnson next door doesn't see it that way, of course. She says she doesn't agree with migrants, whatever that means. She was even saying it when their Andrew wanted to buy that bar in Spain.

Anyway, where was I? I got side-tracked by the ducks. Oh yes, my little shy family. The mother has certainly got them neatly turned out, I must say. But what must that little girl be thinking in these funny times?

This is a strange country to end up in, after a journey like that. We've been on a tractor, we've been on a ship, we've been in a horrible boat, we've even been inside a lorry. Mum and Dad hugged us through it all. Now we're in a place where no-one can touch each other. They come out once a week in our street and start clapping, and even then they don't touch each other. The weather's better than I expected, though. I've not seen much of that rain they kept warning us about.

Jamal is younger than me and I know he finds it a bit frightening here in Wigan. The only time people started to smile was that day they all hung flags up on their houses. They were drinking beer and cooking meat and playing music that I didn't recognise. They didn't smile at us, of course.

Flags are scary. They made Mum start crying again. I think flags remind her of the soldiers back home, and the uniform, and the guns they shot grandma with when we ran away in the night. That's the worst thing that has ever happened to me. I miss grandma and I miss her hugs too, but I remember what she always said. You need to store up enough happiness in the good times to keep you going through the bad.

I want my mum to feel safe, so she won't cry so much. And if this is where we have to stay, my dream is making some friends here in Wigan.

***

If your dad was still alive, Julie, we'd be going over there to talk to that little family, I know we would. Harry would have had the confidence. I'd be showing them how to rub the statue's foot for good luck.
And you know what I'd be wishing for, don't you? A great big hug.

A Month of Sundays: A Requiem for the Life Before the Virus
by Ian McLoughlin

Preamble:

When I was very small, long long ago, when even the eternal golden summers were in black and white, a lot of the books I used to read - and, dear reader (as those self-same books were wont to say) - there were a lot of books, many of them probably not best suited to a child of my tender years, but they often began with a preamble; it's a word I've loved for many years and even now I can see us, you and I, pottering about, getting a few final things together, before we set out on the great journey ... though this particular perambulation, will, I fear, be more of a Sunday afternoon stroll, but hopefully you get my point.

One series of books I used to read and re-read with undiminished glee was the retelling of the Uncle Remus Stories, featuring the mischievous Brer Rabbit, by our very own (and now not exactly in-favour) Enid Blyton. This rather severe, late Victorian lady with her very strict views on the structure of society was responsible for the absorption by my brain of two phrases far removed from her East-Dulwich-based existence: lawksamussy - which I presume is an approximation of a Southern States accented "Lord have mercy!" and the

rather more curious one that often appeared whenever Brer Rabbit caused a problem, as he always did, and swore never to go near the other creatures again for a "month of Sundays" At first, my six year old brain thought "Oh, that's four weeks!" an almost unimaginable stretch of time in my eyes; then I thought of what the Sundays I knew at the time consisted of; very long and very often tedious days, and then the thought struck me - what if what dear old Brer Rabbit actually meant was a whole month where every day was a Sunday - I was shocked and somewhat horrified at this thought. I should point out that in those faraway days there was very little to do on a Sunday except go to church (which we didn't) or dress up in our Sunday best and wait for the arrival of equally bored relatives (which we did); no shops were open, except for florists who furnished us with blooms for our occasional visits to long-dead relatives in the cemetery. A month of Sundays - who can imagine the horror of that?And then we come to now; May 2020 and the lockdown that came into place on the eve of my 60th birthday in March - what dear reader, did I make of that? To find out, read on ...

The Journey Proper Begins:

So I have a bit of a confession to make; I have really enjoyed the lockdown. I know many of you will take exception to that remark, especially the use of the word "enjoy"; I also know that for many people - those who have lost lovedones; or who are struggling for money, or for those keenly missing their friendsand relatives - it's been an horrendous time, and I don't mean to even begin totake any part of their suffering away from them, but for me, personally, it'sbeen a blessing, a benediction. I walk out with my small, elderly dog Sal, two or three times a day, and the streets are more or less deserted. The traffic noise has been replaced with birdsong, the skies feel bigger and clearer, especially now that the very

occasional passing airplane causes one to look up in wonder. At night the silence is deep and, on our late-night, just-before-bed ambles, more oftenthan not we are treated to a crystal clear hemisphere, studded with stars, clearly visible despite the best efforts of the streetlights. The ISS (International Space Station) has been gracing these self-same skies, serenely passing through the confetti shower of the Lyrid meteors; The world feels cleaner, fresher, more untouched.

The world has suddenly been forced to shift gear and engage a slower pace, which is also my pace, and that's why I am enjoying it so much; I find myself hoping that once the world recovers and things get back to normal that we don't - well, get back to normal; at least, not the old normal, but a new more considered and considerate way of being.

Counterintuitively, I've worked and created more in this period of lockdown than I would have thought; the music has flowed, as have the words - obviously, my film making has ground to a halt but that's because filmmaking is a very collaborative process and therefore impossible to carry out under the circumstances - but the rest has been almost supercharged. Of course, no one is buying the words or the music; I don't want you to think I have become a millionaire - or even vaguely solvent - during this period because I very patently haven't; but the meetings in coffee shops have stopped; the travelling to Media City or wherever simply isn't happening, so my expenses have diminished, and, to be honest, I don't miss the meetings or the travelling one bit.

My world has grown smaller.

As often happens with older people, their world shrinks and they become more, if not isolated exactly (though this can be the case), more turned in upon themselves, more reflective, more - to the outside world at least - lost in their own thoughts, and that's me except that I'm not lost; I have a map and am exploring and rediscovering whole long-lost worlds.

One of my very favourite quotes from my favourite writer Virginia Woolf is "A woman must have money and a room of her own if she is to write fiction." and I think this is so true, and not just of women, or of fiction, but for all creative people in all fields. In my case, the world has contracted to the dimensions of a room, my room; the need for external things has diminished and the little money I have is enough to more less get by on. Time has ceased to be as important as we thought it to be and so the creativity flourishes.

And people? What of other people? This is a difficult but not impossible one to answer. Anyone who knows me would probably say I was an outgoing, sociable sort, which is true but only up to a point; I also love being alone.

I can socially chat for hours about anything but prefer depth to my conversations; I'm okay meeting new people but don't like large gatherings, definitely not a party-person. I'm what is termed an "extroverted introvert" which, although seemingly, a contradiction in terms, actually isn't. If you think of a long sliding scale with introvert at 1 and extrovert at 10 I'm probably a 5 ... or sometimes a 3 ... or even a 1 or a 7 ... it changes with the time and circumstances - and lockdown has been a period of exceptional times and strange circumstances.

Lockdown by Molly Burrows

A Month of Sundays: A Requiem for the Life Before the Virus by Ian McLoughlin cont.

I'm lucky in that I have people who I love, and who love me; I know they're 'there' even if they aren't 'here' so I'm okay with that. I know for many people - especially those at 9 or 10 on the extrovert scale this has been a time of great hardship; similarly for those who suffer with anxiety it has been an
unimaginable time of stress and worry. All of this I know but for me, personally, it has been a period of calm reflection and creative bounty. That's me, that's just the way I am and - as Virginia also said:

"It is much more important to be oneself than anything else. Do not dream of
influencing other people...Think of things in themselves."
So what of the Requiem For Life Before The Virus? Well, my month of Sundays
is actually two months now and, despite the protestations of my inner six-year
old, my outer sixty-year is very much at peace with it all.

Of course, I'm angry with the way it has been handled. I'm saddened beyond belief at the very often unnecessary suffering and death brought about because of ideology and what I believe to be self-interest on behalf of our leaders.

I'm also happy that, so far at least, I'm still alive; and that I continue to creatively extract the sweetness and goodness out of what is undoubtedly a terrible situation.

A Month of Sundays: A Requiem for the Life Before the Virus by Ian McLoughlin cont.

Epilogue

I'll end with an extract from a book I read much later in life, when I was in my mid-twenties and, consequently knew even less about life than I did at six.

"Lavengro: The Scholar, the Gypsy, the Priest" is a work by George Borrow, and falls somewhere between the genres of memoir and novel. According to the author "lavengro" is a Romany word meaning "word master" and the book features many conversations between the protagonist George, who has given up his job and taken to the road as a tinker, and the various Romany folk he encounters. Here he sits at a campfire at night.

"Life is sweet, brother."
"Do you think so?"
"Think so!—There's Night and Day,
Brother, both sweet things.
Sun, Moon, and Stars, Brother -
All sweet things -
And there's the wind on the heath, Brother.
Who would wish to die..."
from "Lavengro" by George Borrow, 1851

Ian McLoughlin MBKS is a writer, composer and filmmaker based in Wigan.

Covid-19 Lockdown
by Anita Fazackerley

At first, the terror. The unknown. The unfamiliarity. The vulnerability. Then we settled, accepted and waited. We'd been at The Courts only a few weeks ago watching the Bowie tribute, the virus then just a distant thrum on the radio, something happening in other countries. How things changed, and so quickly.

Schools. Colleges. Then pubs, restaurants and non-essential businesses. The gravity of the closings began to awaken every sleeping nerve. Then it burgeoned into queues everywhere, with shortages of basic items becoming commonplace as panic seeped through the veins of every household consumer.

There were lots of random acts of kindness too. The woman who gave me one of the last two tubes of tomato puree she had just put in her own trolley so I wouldn't be without. A neighbour who shared out bread flour then we scoured the shops and waited patiently until yeast could be had and shared, then baking could begin.

The elderly neighbours who waved as we went past and sometimes mouthed or held aloft handwritten signs in their windows when they needed things from the shop as they knew we could (and did) replenish their stocks.

Choking with emotion, I silently stifled sobs as the daffodils planted in my garden as a memorial to someone indelibly inked on my heart poked through the ground in an act of soundless reassurance. Usually this annual spring event would thrill me, and I would revel in the memories it evoked and the wonder of new life bursting from the ground. So different this time. However, the strangest of all was yet to come - the funeral of my quiet, kind, gentle Uncle, with five mourners sat in the service at the regulatory measure of 2 metres apart. No touching, no consoling of each other, no congregation, no limousine, no wake; the fondest and most tender of eulogies desperately trying to compensate for the dire lack of permitted mourners and the usual post-service celebration of his life.
I hope he understands.

Outside, at home, the quiet. In the evenings, sat in the garden bathed in unexpected – nay, miraculous – blazing April sunshine, I sat and heeded my partner's soft
breathing, a steady and comforting rhythm uninterrupted by the usual punctuation of airplane traffic or cars returning the workers from their daily grind. The sun stroked my skin lazily as I observed him, eyes closed, long, blond eyelashes sweeping his smooth cheeks, countenance perfectly peaceful, and mouthed a silent prayer giving thanks that he and my son were safe, as were his daughter and partner, mother, my dad, my friends and other family. Would it always be so? Who knew? I pushed the terrible thought back deep into the furthermost cavern in my mind, but, like an oversized jack-in-the-box, it would bound right back out again, especially in the early hours of the mornings.
I ached to hug my son again too, my beautiful son who works hundreds of miles away and whose baby-smell I can still recall in an instant. He's 25 now, but that sensation doesn't lessen.

We What's-Apped and phoned and video-connected, but sometimes the distance felt unbearable. What if something happened to him? What if he became ill and I wasn't allowed to visit him? What if I never saw him again? Down, jack-in-the-box, down. I forced it down harder. It remained in the box. For now.

Daily, the birds celebrated their pollution-less air by singing for all they were worth, their higher and lower-pitched notes drifting across the air and tickling our ears like the tiny breeze from a butterfly's wings. So welcome, that sound. We admired them as they darted in and out of hedges, their optimism never failing as they collected a mass of little
treasures with which to build their nests.
Life goes on.

Unfailingly, we clapped and banged, tambourined and waved on Thursdays at 8pm too, to thank the NHS staff who were working so incredibly hard for us all. That was the weekly glimmer of hope, the sense of community, the shared experience, the idea that this situation would, one day, cease.

And, as the Captain Toms of this world raised money by all kinds of ingenious means to support the NHS, and people made PPE, delivered food parcels, donated to the food banks, volunteered for the NHS, helped their neighbours and a myriad of other acts of selflessness and kindness abounded, it became clear that the overarching feeling was that we could weather the storm if we braved the waves together.

As, occasionally, the storm threatened to wash me overboard, the lines of the Verve song which has hauled me through so many challenges over the years, but which has never felt more poignant than at present, leapt from my sound system and urged me to "Tie yourself to the mast, my friend, and the storm will end." Yes. One day the storm will break and there will be a semblance of normality. One day I will warm from the touch and smiles of family and friends again. One day this will be over. I'm still waiting.

Floating Through Chaos
by Dean Baggaley

You think you might have the symptoms
You're wrong I hope, there's already real victims.

You're worried about incomes?
Our worries about incomes depend upon the continuation of our international systems.

It's time the generations stepped up,
Regardless of age and politics we need to make up.

At last we can show some solidarity,
Some charity, aspire some clarity through this barbarity, this messed up disparity, this austerity,
show some calm through the hilarity.. despite its severity.

The borders are closed and we are afraid,
This is a global catastrophic clustered grenade.

The pin has been pulled but it's not too late,
To show some love to thy neighbor, rather than hate.

Think about that old man, think about your friends, think about those you can help when you're
picking from the shelf,
Because in these times, you might just need it yourself.

Now is absolutely the time, to work together for the love of humanity,
Because none of us have any immunity.

The Day the World Stopped by Jessica Anderton

The day the world stopped
And time stood still,
The day the world slowed
But the Carers still showed,
The day the world paused
And at 8 we applause,
The day the world gloomed
Some bang saucepans and spoons,
The day the world watched
Netflix & Disney, updates at 5 o'clock,
The day the world waited
Children proud of rainbows they'd painted,
The day the world distanced
But some didn't listen,
The day the world prayed
For Borris, all the plans he had made,
The day the world blamed
But there was noone to blame,

The day the world dualed
And the parents homeschooled,
The day the world paid
Our hero Tom walked all day,
The day the world shut
And the wages got cut,
The day the world hoped
That our health service could cope,
The day the world played
But in our gardens we stayed,
The day the world cried
But the nurses, they tried,
The day the world stopped
And time stood still,
But better days they came
And the world smiled again...

The Invaders by Jill Norris

Thirteen nights ago my body was invaded.
They have no name, but I know they`re there.
Into my bloodstream and veins they waded,
Intent on doing damage wherever they were.

My throat was attacked and my sinuses too;
My head was plugged tight with wool.
I coughed and I hacked all the night through,
They carried on coming like a raging bull.

Now they are here and in full control,
Weakness prevents my defense.
Tapping away at my mind and my soul,
Nothing I do makes sense.

They hammer away in my woody head,
They attack the throat with knives.
They fill my stomach with bile and lead,
They`re immune to my pleas and cries.

They wake me when I fall asleep
With hacking coughs and pain.
They revel in my need to weep;
They`re killing me grain by grain.

Thirteen nights ago my body was invaded.
They have no name, but I know they`re there.
Into my bloodstream and veins they waded,
Intent on doing damage wherever they were.

My throat was attacked and my sinuses too;
My head was plugged tight with wool.
I coughed and I hacked all the night through,
They carried on coming like a raging bull.

Now they are here and in full control,
Weakness prevents my defense.
Tapping away at my mind and my soul,
Nothing I do makes sense.

They hammer away in my woody head,
They attack the throat with knives.
They fill my stomach with bile and lead,
They`re immune to my pleas and cries.

They wake me when I fall asleep
With hacking coughs and pain.
They revel in my need to weep;
They`re killing me grain by grain.

Locked Down by John Dykhuizen

Oh we get along
Oh sometimes it's wrong
Theres nothing to do around here
Your friends and your neighbours to be feared
You cant always do what you've done
That's not how the west is won

But when I look back on it
Did you take just what you wanted
Will we remember when these are the things

Oh we get along
Theres nothing to do around here
The word from up high is still unclear
People furloughed at home
I'll be working alone

But when we look back on it
Did you do just what you wanted
Will we remember when these are the things

The Vixen and the Virus Moon by John Jarvis

She'll be there,
a blink away from the dark.
Follow her,
if you can,
away from the little park.
Take care down by the tracks,
where life is taken
in the passing of an hour.
Take your torch
and slyly watch which way she goes-
across the down fast,
or on to the up slow.
This virus moon is bright tonight,
which may help her on her way.
But take heed at the junction's cross,
or you'll let her get
away!

Lockdown Love Is...... by Karen Thompson

Lockdown love is losing my Mum, how I never saw this coming,
Lockdown love is missing my Granddaughter like nobody would believe
Oh how it hurts!
Lockdown love is sharing family time on zoom, so grateful to technology.
Lockdown love is working through challenges, categorically.
Lockdown love is facing fear with hope, grit and gratitude,
Lockdown love is praying for the change in societies attitudes.
Lockdown love is unique and may never rise again,
Lockdown love is me and me I will remain.

What Was It Like Mum? by Laura Mullard

One day, one day will come, you will turn to me and ask so mum....

What was it like that covid 19? All I remember is it being sunny and upbeat.

We had time to play and laugh and have fun, you and dad never made it feel glum.

Well kids here is the thing, we were scared but it made us all sing.
We danced around the room and made some tik toks, although dad hates to admit his dance moves really suck.

We clapped at our doors every Thursday at 8, to thank all the key workers and to pray they keep safe.

At this time the world stood so still, it made us thankful for our health and good will.

I'm scared I'm not a teacher and you won't learn new things, but that's ok we will learn some life skills.

So we walked, and baked and snuggled together for this is the time we will remember forever.

So yes we were scared, and sad and frightened but this time in our h mo lives made us all enlightened.

One thing is for sure we will never take for granted, the love for others the hugs that we planted.

Unspoken by Maire Robinson

During Covid-19
We sat
And watched TV
As usual
Holding hands
A little bit tighter than before

Their Lockdown by Mandie Biggs

My girls miss your birthdays,
but celebrated ours.
They miss going in your garden,
and watering your flowers.
They cry saying goodbye on the phone,
they do not understand why we are at home.
But we play, bake and have fun,
When the little one eats paint,
And they are fairies in the sun.
They have good days and bad,
But they are safe at home,
With Mum and Dad.

By your Mummy

Lockdown Through The Eyes of a Depressed Disabeld Diabetic
by Margaret Wood

For me lockdown hasn't changed a bit, due to various incidents over the last 10 years I've ended up in a wheelchair.

So, for eight years I was in semi isolation as my husband was working as School Crossing Patrolman and lunch time supervisor so I could not go out by myself and was only going out at weekends and school holidays. He has now been retired for three years, but unfortunately in 2017 he was diagnosed with head and neck cancer, for which he was treated at the MRI and Christie and has been now been given the all clear. So, when lockdown started it was like me welcoming people to my world.

We were able to go birdwatching and holidays which resulted in me kissing an Alpaca. Now the highlight of the week is going out to a large Supermarket, but we are in and out in 15 minutes. Birdwatching is out as reserves etc have all be closed. So now we just sit in our front garden, if the weather permits it, making silly plans of what we would be going to do. The downside is because I know that we cannot go out I want to.

Hopefully we are going on holiday in late September, in the UK, and hopefully I'll be catching up with my Alpaca friends.

But looking on the bright side we are both living and have a future to look forward to.

Thank You
by Maria Byrne

Thank you NHS for fixing my dad,
Thanks for saving my brothers life,
And giving a ♥,
Thanks for trying to save my mother,
Even though you didn't succeed,
I saw you try,
Thank you for,
Fighting a virus,
With no battle protection,
And mostly with,
Bare hands,
Strength,
Thank you for all,
Who are here,
To save lives every day,
And thanks to all the key workers,
Who go out to work,
And those who work from home,
Thank you,
To all the creative people,
Who set our minds at rest at night,
And see us through the day,
Thank you to the friends,
That support each other,
Through isolating times,
Thank you to each other.

Isolation Deprivations
by Natasha Tingle

We're all in the same situation,
So you'll know the things I miss.
The sweet twisted pleasure gone out of life.
It's hard to encounter the bounty of nature,
Those melt-on-your-tongue flakes of moments
Drawn from unpredictable people,
Their utterings and mutterings and mixups.
We are awakened to the zesty mystery
We had such unaware access to before:
An aeronautic twirl betwixt light and dark;
Ancient minstrels with flutes declaring
The cosmic egg of chaos mingled among us,
Invisible millions against the very God of war, Mars.
Our plight births a boost to examine our origins,
Our curling galaxy, the Milky Way,
On a small Button Moon scale.
It has made us have a break and laugh together,
Or perhaps snicker at one another,
But laugh all the same.
But how profoundly we miss it,
Like a whispered lion's roar
Oozing and rippling into our awareness.
Yes, we are all in the same situation.
Not enough chocolate!

Gifts During Third Week of April
by Sue Lewis

I was in the kitchen on the phone to my sister. I looked out of the window towards the gate, a delivery driver in a mask and gloves was waving to me. No, he wasn't delivering some dangerous chemicals or a new born baby it was a plain cardboard box about the size of a small pizza box only deeper. I put down the phone and went to the gate. Through his mask he asked me my name and address. This was as i was rubbing on hand sanitiser gel.

I thanked him, keeping the recommended safe distance and carried the box inside. luckily it was wrapped in plastic. I carefully sprayed it with anti bacterial spray and wiped it with kitchen roll which I immediately put in the bin. I once again gelled my hands then opened the box.It was a gift from The New England Cookie Company. I decided to wash my hands with soap and water as as it was food I didn't want it tasting of anti bacterial gel.

Inside was an assortment of cookies, salted caramel,chocolate chip,fruit shortbread and orange and chocolate flavours. it was a gift from my son and his partner. Inside there was a note it said""hope we can soon all sit down and share cookies and coffee"" together

A tear slid down my cheek, they only live around the corner."

I Am Not Alone I Know by Susan Rigby

I am not alone I know
But my feelings tear me apart
I have a sense of guilt
But my feelings tear me apart
When will it end this conflict we are in
But my feelings tear me apart
It is misleading sometimes the news
But my feelings tear me apart
Can't seem to get started
My feelings are tearing me apart
I am shredded to the bone
Tearing me apart my feelings
Come on stand up be brave
Feelings are part of you
You are not alone
Your feelings are you
I stand innocent I know.

Earth Rest Is Our Test by Terry Burtonwood

Blackpool seas; clear blue
Instead of dirty grey
Wildlife's returning
Instead of hiding away

The earths resting
Pollution isn't there
It's taken a deadly virus
To give us all a scare

Let's pray when it's all over
Lessons have been learned
The chance to make a difference
Hasn't been spurned

Let's do it for the ones we lost
The ones we had to sacrifice
So that future generations
Won't have to pay the price."

A Spring Day in Whelley by Anna Croxall

Second Walk by Thomas Jones

Second Walk

the sky is clearer
people are nearer
despite being further away
less trails in the sky
only the clunk of DIY coming from the garden next door

more bright dots in the dark,
brown bins overflow,
a shared momentary lapse in the undertow

quieter roads, trucks carrying lighter loads -
the birds reclaiming the sky

online quizzers indulge in conspiracy talk
as they lay back in garden chairs
considering the risks of a second walk

much has wilted and much has thrived
what a genuinely strange time to be alive

That's Okay by Thomas Jones

I write, sing, and play
In the quiet fear I won't remember how to — when finally refacing an audience.
My longest absence from performance since being a child,
only canned applause and laughter remains.
The sound bites of the passed .
I wonder how many artists went live that first weekend of lockdown just out of habit , it's
Saturday it's 8 30 pm and it's time to perform just like every other weekend -
isn't it ?
Pixelated solace & validation
in the warm yellow embrace of a clapping emoji, you will have to do,
for now.
I recalled hearing about a dog that went on the same walk his owner took him on everyday for
a whole year after the passing of its owner as i shared my video in a last minute dashed attempt
to increase its post reach. Do people even want this? am i spam now?

Writing is hard although i have the time.

We could all do the things we always wanted to but never had the time to
but we won't and that's okay .

The Lockdown by Tom Walsh

Lockdown, a word we'd never heard before, a world we'd never known.
Who could have thought to hug a loved one would be tantamount to sin.
That Thursday night at eight o'clock would be the highlight of the week.
Parted from the ones we love with an imaginary wall two metres thick
New heroes to honour we have found aplenty ,our gratitude we must show.

When this nightmare ends as one day this will be ,what matters we will surely know.

Material things will lose their lustre, love will overcome the stoutest of the stoutest wall.
To be again in union, to hold hands of those you love will seem a dream come true!

A Lad From Scholes Meets Queen Victoria by Tom Walsh

During the lockdown I've spent some of my walks in Wigan Cemetery (no trouble with social distancing),on one walk I spotted the grave of Robert Richards - the inscription read Mayor of Wigan .I couldn't resist finding out more, and his is a fascinating story - taking him from Scholes to Buckingham Palace. Robert's early life had not been easy. He was born in Wallgate in 1831, the family moved to Scholes presumably be to near to his maternal Grandparents, his Grandfather was licensee of The Harp' , this public house was to play a major part in his later life. He was educated at St. Catherine School sadly his mother died when Robert was just 7 years old.

The following is brief look at his story.

In 1890s there were over 60 Public houses in the Scholes area alone not mention Umpteen others across the borough, my Father was born in such an establishment "The Kings Arms." However the story is centred on one particular pub on the Scholes thoroughfare itself "The Harp" and its Landlord Robert Richards.who was to serve as Wigan Mayor for 2 consecutive terms and whilst a Conservative himself, I doubt if he thought he would be mentioned in the same breath as Sir Randolph Churchill, Sir Winston Churchill's father. Sir Randolph had made a speech (House of Commons 1892)on the dangers of alcohol calling everything concerned with the trade as devilish, strange, when both he and his son enjoyed a tipple or three!

Robert Richards was the licensee of The Harp at the time of his Mayorship , because he was involved in the licensing trade, he was the first man from that trade to become Mayor, his appointment however wasn't welcomed by everyone particularly the temperance movement ,and many mainly from the nonconformist churches objected.

A Lad From Scholes Meets Queen Victoria by Tom Walsh cont.

Robert himself was a prominent member of nearby St. Catherine's Church but this did nothing to stop the criticism .The significance of Robert's position did not go unnoticed outside borough either, Rev.C F Alked a nonconformist Minister delivered a sermon in Preston on 31st October 1897 primarily against the appointment of the Lord Mayor of Liverpool who like Robert Richards was involved in the licensing trade. he said in his sermon particularly regarding Liverpool where protests were being voiced in response to the similar situation of a "brewer and publican" being proposed to fulfill the post of next Lord Mayor of Liverpool. During the sermon he urged the churches of Liverpool to boycott their proposed Lord Mayor saying that "the city would never disgrace themselves by allowing a liquor seller to preside over their meetings".

The Reverend Gentleman continued his sermon, referring to the quote by Sir Randolph Churchill which had called the liquor business a devilish and destructive trade, he continued by saying that decent people could not help but be ashamed that a man engaged in such a trade had been engineered into the mayoral chair,

as a consequence of which Liverpool would become contemptible in the eyes of the great cities of England. He proceeded this by a tirade against our town -" The second city of the empire had fallen to the level of WIGAN, and like that drink cursed town had found its chief magistrate is a publican".

I ought to explain at that time anyone elected Mayor automatically became a magistrate. Robert Richards first term in office 1897 was to be very eventful this was the year of Queen Victoria's Diamond Jubilee .On 23rd June 1897 he attended Buckingham Palace and was formally presented to her. Six days after meeting Queen Victoria he was presented to and dined with, the Duke of York. The following March 1898 during his second term of office, had the honour of being presented to the Prince of Wales (later to become King Edward VII) this was during the Prince's visit to stay at Garswood Hall the home of the Prince's friend Lord Gerard, not bad going for a lad brought up in Scholes!

In 1897 Robert also played a part in one of the biggest retailers in the country he and the then   Chief of Police Captain Bell gave a character reference in   connection Michael Marks application for naturalisation as result of their intervention it was granted on the 5th of May 1897. Marks & Spencer owe to much to Wigan , Michael Marks lived in Wigan at152 Great George Street one of one of his children born at that address.Interesting he had signed the birth Certificate an' X '.

Michael Marks started the business in Leeds when he went into partnership with Tom Spencer it was during his time in Wigan So I think it's fair to claim that the business in its extended form was actually born in Wigan. Another gravestone brought a lump to my throat, it wouldn't be fair to revel the names but   the inscription mentions the names followed by "WITH LOVE AND THANKS TO MY ADOPTED PARENTS "

It looks a knew stone and the parents mentioned have been dead for many years . There is an old Lancashire saying "Eaten bread is soon forgotten "   However this inscription says to me " love never dies "

I much prefer that sentiment .

Stupid Earth People by Paula Clarkson

The people they gathered in
masses and masses
In pubs and in clubs they were filling their glasses
Whilst death lay in wait, so silent unseen
A name on his lips whispered Covid-19

And millions of people we sit and we wait
For death to come calling
And sealing our fate

And death keeps on creeping and wringing his hands
The stupid earth people all part of his plans.
You just wouldn't listen, you just didn't care
You must keep your distance stay indoors, beware

And millions of people we sit and we wait
For death to come calling
And sealing our fate

But stupid earth people thought they knew the best
The Government warnings they're only in jest.
And death is still waiting, his scythe held up high
You've used all your chances, it's too late to cry.

And millions of people still sit and still wait
For death WILL come calling
And sealing our fate

Forget You Not by Samantha Turner

I know you are afraid my friend
The world is suddenly strange
There is a real threat of danger
And life out there has changed

Do you have everything you need my friend
Can I help in any way?
Not just with doorstep drop offs
Or words through window pane

For sustenance is more
Than merely bread and tea
What about the laughter?
The chats and memories?

When all of this is over
And survivors come outdoors
To celebrate with family
Not take for granted anymore

The liberty and open space
The birdsong and the sky
Maybe will mean much more to us
The joy we cannot buy

The streets will all be bustling
The parks all filled with play
The world will seem much brighter
Through eyes which once were grey

With gratitude and huge relief
That danger is averted
Life will pour upon the world
No city still deserted

But what becomes of you my friend?
Still trapped inside your home
The illness may have passed for us
Yet for you it is the norm

For you are old and shaky
Alone since Mary passed
Just a photo on the mantelpiece
You smile and she smiles back

My friend will they remember you
Still watching through the glass?
Will greed and self-return again
Will kindness walk on past?

I don't want you to worry friend
For lessons have been learned
You will never be forgotten
Or left alone and scared

Can you hear me now my friend?
I'm knocking on your door
There's a party in the street outside
Let me help you get your coat!

Coming Back by Samantha Turner

I'm coming back to you
When all of this is done
Even if the seasons changed
And leaves are golden brown
If Summer time means solitude
Alone in gardens bare
I'll get my warmth from sunshine
And conversation from the birds
Don't dwell on all the sadness
Or all the things we've missed
The earth is merely resting
Taking time to deal with this
I'm coming back to you
We all just need to wait
To heed the constant warning
Stay home. Stay safe.

March 2020 by Sandra Stuart

Go for a walk
Or maybe a run
But on our own -
It can still be fun -
We can party together
When all this is done

Whether we're struggling
Or have lots of wealth
This virus can attack us
Silently and in stealth
Especially the elderly
And those in ill-health
We MUST think of others
And not just ourself

All over the world
Literally everywhere
We must shield and protect
And show that we care
Not be greedy or selfish
But generous and share
Our time for a phone call
Acts of kindness here and there

Volunteer if we're able
To help others who are not
But stay indoors mainly
Even if it's sunny and hot
It's not asking too much
It's not asking a lot
To safeguard our loved ones
And all that we've got

Our doctors and nurses
In our great NHS
Working on the frontline
With all the worry and stress
Our Carers and all key workers
I have to confess
I've never been so grateful
That they're here through this mess

So lets all work with them
It won't be easy or fast
But when we beat this
Together, what a contrast!
When it's all over
And the virus has passed
You can come and share our view
And I can hug you at last

When Life Changed Spring 2020 by Sheila Hinds

Our country is in lockdown! This means we must stay at home. People must work from home, if possible. Schools are closed, except for the children of key workers (hospital staff and care workers). Employees have been 'furloughed' - a word I hadn't known before. In a nutshell, they have been 'layed off'. The government has agreed to pay 80% of their wages. Many people are affected by this. The only shops open are food shops for essentials and chemists. I keep hearing this phrase: "We are living in unprecedented times."

This is Great Britain in April 2020. The world is in the midst of a contagious virus that has proved deadly to thousands of people throughout the world.

Our Government is barraging us with instructions: 'Stay at home! No social gatherings! Do not see family or friends! Go outside for exercise, just once a day!'

I commence my daily walk, thankful that the sun is not dissuaded by this polluted planet it sees below. Looking up through shaded eyes, I see an infinite mass of pale blue cloudless sky. There are no aeroplanes streaming their way to faraway destinations. It's hard not to believe that this is just a perfect day.

The birdsong sounds heavenly in the deathly quiet streets. The little front lawns have been mowed and the sweet scent of newly cut grass is kissing my nostrils. People are giving the fence a new coat of paint, trimming their trees and hedges. They're catching up on all the jobs they never seem to have time for in their busy working lives.

Flowers of all colours are putting on a tantalising show, as they dance in the faintest breeze. Daffodils, Tulips, Dahlias, Camelias, all bursting with the spring fever of new life. I yearn to feel the same energy travel through my body, fortifying my soul and lifting my spirits. Nature continues to replenish and revitalise the earth. If this phenomenon ever ceases, then man will surely be responsible for its demise.

As I continue down the road I notice so many cars sitting motionless, like redundant road furniture. Their journeys suspended, as so many people are away from work and schools are closed.

Social Distancing by Sarah Louise Hind

Jess took a seat on a bench at the edge of the now-closed play park; the only activity was a magpie wrestling with a discarded bread roll. Suddenly the thought of going back to that house was a little more than she was ready to cope with right now.

Her gran had taught her to always count the blessings first. A nice house. A nice car.

Nice holidays. Nice food. Money to do nice things.

Nice. Nice. Nice.

She wanted more than nice. The problem was that she didn't know that 'more' was.

We have a nice little routine going to be honest. The kids are feral but they're learning a lot and we're enjoying each other's company. You know those families who just quit their jobs and go on the road with the kids and the dog and live out of a camper van for five years? I feel like that's us right now. Only, you know, without the travelling." Karen paused for breath and sipped her gin slowly. She missed her sister so much but honestly, this more relaxed lockdown life was a blessing. She didn't have to have her constantly hanging around the house, taking the mick out of her husband and moaning that the kids were too loud.

"Right. Yeah we've got a similar situation here, only without the kids or the dog. But, do you not feel sort of...I don't know.

Trapped?" Jess also sipped her gin, mildly irritated with the condensation from the glass sliding over her fingers.

"Do you mean physically? Or mentally?"

"Both. Mentally. Like, this has just highlighted everything you knew was wrong but didn't want to admit? Martin is a right pain in the arse, you must be tearing your hair out with him hanging around all day." Jess didn't really love or loathe her sister's husband, merely tolerated his wanna-be-hipster dad fashion, unfunny jokes and his constant need to be the centre of attention.

"No, Jess. This has highlighted all the reasons we got together in the first place." Karen sighed loudly and drained her glass before carrying on. "Look, we got together and fell in love and sure, having kids and a business and a mortgage and dad dying and all those other things are stressful, but being in lockdown has forced us to spend time together. We're so busy usually, and when we're busy we're tired and stressed and we get snappy and we stop talking to each other. We just maintain the status quo of getting the kids to school and walking the dog and...well just life crap. It's existing. Now I feel like we're living."

"Right."

Olly Sibbit (Aged 9)

Wigan Lockdown I am very bored
due to the current situation.
I am missing my friends from school
and looking forward to seeing them again.
I miss hugging my baby cousin, and building with my grandad John.

Paul Southward

Given all the horrible sad loss and scary times I can't help thinking there
was something mind blowing and beautiful about how the human race can
come together and get through whatever is thrown in front of them in this life.
Beautiful!

Printed in Great Britain
by Amazon